DENEBI

Farmstead of the Danes

A History of Upper & Lower Denby
by
Chris Heath

ISBN 1 872955 19 3

First published in 1997
by
Richard Netherwood Limited
539 Manchester Road
Huddersfield

Printed by Dearneside Press, Scissett

Dedication

For my Dad, with love and thanks.

Acknowledgements

Grateful thanks must be given to the following, without whom this book would have been significantly thinner:

Jim Barber, Frank & Lynn Burdett, Stella Crossland, Doug & June Fisher, John Gaunt, John Goodchild, Bryan Heath, Carol Heath, Paul Heath, Ronald Heath, Harry Heath, Annie Heath, Jane Helliwell (Huddersfield Local History Library), Stella Kenyon, Rupert Gill Martin, Christine Martin, Ava Newby, Lena Nicholson, Phillip Parker, Margaret Peace, Richard Peace, Mabel Pickford, Joe Price, John Rumsby (Curator, Tolson Museum, Huddersfield), W H Senior, Steven and Jill Slater, Karen Smith, Betty Springer, John White, Johnny White, David & Keeley Whittaker, George Wilby.

And finally, a special mention for the historians, now passed away, who not only provided the foundation for my work but also the inspiration;

John Dransfield, Rev. Joseph Hunter, Fred Lawton, and Henry Moorhouse.

Any errors or omissions in this book are entirely my own therefore none of the above should be chided into responsibility.

Forefathers.

Here they went with smock and crook,
Toiled in the sun, lolled in the shade,
Here they muddied out the brook
And here their hatchet cleared the glade:
Harvest supper woke their wit,
Huntsman's moon their wooings lit.

From this church they led their brides,
From this church they themselves were led
Shoulder-high ; on these waysides
Sat to take their beer and bread.
Names are gone - what men they were
These their cottages declare.

Names are vanished, save the few
In the old brown Bible scrawled;
They were men of pith and thew,
Whom the city never called;
Scarce could read or hold a quill,
Built the barn, the forge, the mill.

On the green they watched their sons
Playing till too dark to see,
As their fathers watched them once,
As my father once watched me;
While the bat and beetle flew,
On warm air webbed with dew.

Unrecorded, unreknowned,
Men from whom my ways begin,
Here I know you by your ground
But I know you not within -
There is silence, there survives
Not a moment of your lives.

Like the bee that now is blown
Honey - heavy on my hand,
From his toppling tansy-throne
In the green tempestuous land
I'm in clover now, nor know
Who made honey long ago.

Edmund Blunden.

INTRODUCTION

The worlds of family history and local history have been likened to an 'inter changeable jigsaw puzzle, without any straight edges', and constantly missing various important pieces or having pieces which don't fit.

This book is a by product of my research into my own family, who by their close connections with Denby and its environs caused me to look into the background of the settlement to help understand how they lived, loved and died. This was the acorn.

Unfortunately all previously published material was disjointed and fragmentary, sometimes ambiguous and always insufficient. What I needed was a book solely concerned with the settlement, which included all the important previously published material and the fruits of my own enquiries presented in a logical, cohesive, and accessible narrative. The Rev. Joseph Hunter was the first to attempt the task, back in the mid nineteenth century. His work has formed the basis for all subsequent historical research into the village, including that of John Ness Dransfield, who reproduced, word for word, Hunters narrative, adding only his own notes concerning Denby workhouse.

Fred Lawton's notes on the Spanish Armada, the District Militia and Witchcraft added to the tale. Finally William H. Senior has continued the task to this day, adding notable features from the nineteenth and early twentieth century and frequently giving lectures utilising his excellent memory to continue to breath life into this ancient foundation. The work of these four men inspired me to attempt to learn not only all that they knew, but to build on their discoveries and attempt to write the 'logical, cohesive and accessible narrative' that I required.

The book begins in the late Stoneage period, with the settlement at High Flatts, which in historical terms is only a stones throw from the village. Although this chapter appears at first glance to be a fairly general overview of the country up until the Norman Conquest, it does form a pivotal role in setting the scene for the rest of my narrative. For instance, to be able to understand that the site which was to become Denby formed part of the ancient lands known as Elmet, and subsequently part of Northumbria, I believe it prudent to know why these two ancient Kingdoms existed at all.

In essence it would be very difficult to prove that there was any activity on the site of the village before the coming of the 'Vikings' in the ninth century. Yet there must have been tribes living locally and familiar with the topography of the lands here before that time. Further evidence from this 'Dark Age' is unlikely, unless serious archaeological excavation is undertaken in the future, therefore it is down to individual speculation as to the truth of the site before historical documentation.

Cumberworth, and Burnt Cumberworth are both ancient British settlements and are on the boundaries of the present day villages of Upper and Lower Denby. Do they have connections with the settlement on Castle Hill at High Flatts?, were the lands at Denby used by them for hunting?, or was there a settlement here before 'Viking' activity?. Speculative conversation can realise some quite wonderful possibilities!

The narrative moves on from 1066 to the first settlement of the Lords of the Manor, the Burdet's who from at least the thirteenth century until 1643 raised the villages stature and instituted the basis for the modern village of today. Throughout this time and the following 150 years I have endeavoured to intermingle their story with the available details of the lives of the peasants that worked on their lands. Of course, once we reach the nineteenth century a rich wealth of source material still survives to provide a far more detailed picture of the lives of these ordinary folk.

The chapters concerning occupation and leisure and celebration span both the nineteenth and twentieth centuries, and reduce the content in the chapter on the twentieth century by a large degree. Though I believe the narrative in these chapters sits comfortably together.

The book is somewhat 'introverted', much has already been written concerning Denby Dale and Penistone, therefore I was determined to concentrate my attention on the villages of Upper and Lower Denby, both sadly neglected in most modern publications.

In recent years the pursuit of Local History as a pastime has grown immensely and judging by the amount of books available and locally organised lectures and exhibitions I believe that the time is now right for Denby to have at least its first, certainly not the last, history of its own.

Contents

EARLY ORIGINS

The village unit now known as Denby was probably first created soon after the Viking invasion of York in 866 AD. Denby, or Denebi means simply; 'Farmstead of the Danes'. Whether this name was created by the Viking settlers or was given to the village by neighbouring Anglo Saxons is now impossible to tell.

Fortunately the history of the locality stretches back somewhat further and we are able to trace Iron Age and possibly Neolithic (late Stoneage) settlement in and around what is referred to in the 'National Sites and Monuments' record as an 'Iron Age Hill Fort' on Castle Hill at High Flatts.

TABLE OF EARLY TIME PERIODS

MESOLITHIC	(middle stoneage)	8000 BC - 4000 BC
NEOLITHIC	(late stoneage)	4000 BC - 2200 BC
BRONZE AGE		2200 BC - 650 BC
IRON AGE		650 BC - 43 AD
ROMAN		43AD - 410 AD

The modern area of Yorkshire was once part of a much greater territory populated by the ancient British Celtic tribe known as the Brigantes. These were not only warrior people but also skilled craftsmen and traders. Gone were the 'hunter gatherers' of the Stone and Bronze ages, these people now farmed the land and kept livestock for subsistence and made pottery and metalwork, not only for themselves but also for export to the continent. The tribes most famous daughter was Queen Cartimandua, who allowed her kingdom to become a client of Rome during their conquest of the country. She surrendered her countryman, Caratacus to them after he was defeated in battle resisting the Romans and had fled to her for shelter in AD51.

Although it makes sense to mention her in the context of this chapter, it would be a romantic notion to connect her with Denby's modest earthwork. These Britons before the Romans were linked by a more or less common Celtic language which is the ancestor of today's Welsh and Cornish.

It is generally accepted that it is from this group of people that we owe the construction of the High Flatts 'Iron Age Fort', but can this be challenged?

The 'Victoria County History of Britain' suggests that the site is of, 'not exactly a defensive situation' and Henry Moorhouse in his 'History of Kirkburton' was able to suggest only that the earthworks were probably of British origin (though he was writing before excavations were carried out). In 1971 the site, (which is 1025 feet above sea level) was excavated by John Gilks of the Tolson Museum, Huddersfield, though he was not the first to dig here. I have been told of local teachers taking classes onto the hill and setting about it with shovels! Archaeology hasn't always been the science it is today. Also in 1845 a stone axe head was recovered from the property of Herbert Dickinson of High Flatts by workmen labouring on a new drain. Described by Henry Moorhouse as a 'British Celt' (or stone battle axe) it weighed two pounds nine ounces and measured nearly seven inches long, 3 ½ inches on the cutting edge tapering to approximately 2 inches.

Gilks excavations were more controlled and his results illuminating. Circa 90 Neolithic flints were recovered, 80% of which were collected from a 14 square metre area of the plough reduced rampart on the south side of the enclosure. Two fragments of stone axe heads were also found. Flint is not found locally, therefore it was brought here by human hands, upon this basis it is reasonable to assume that the site had Neolithic origins, which could give an earliest date of 4000-2200 BC, for activity in the area. The site itself lies on the southern side of a low hill and the remains extant today have been greatly reduced by ploughing. According to the West Yorkshire Archaeology Service, a slight lowering of the inner bank on

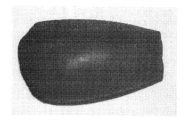

*A typical example of an axe head similar to the ones
discovered at High Flatts (now in a private collection).*

the west side may have been an entrance, but this could also have been caused by cattle! What is almost immediately apparent is the sites poor defensive position. It is overlooked from both the North and East and would have afforded scant protection to its inhabitants against a strong external attack, even with a 3 to 4 metre wide ditch below the ramparts and a strong wooden palisade around the top perimeter.

It would appear more likely that the area was a settlement rather than an 'out and out' military fort, probably a Neolithic site in origin which was re-fortified and occupied by the people of the Iron Age and probably abandoned as the Roman legions were spreading North in their invasion of Britain, and local inhabitants fled to safer strongholds.

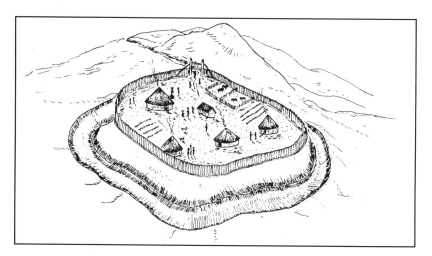

Reconstruction of a fortified Iron Age Hill Fort.

Two other local sites, contemporary with the settlement at High Flatts should be mentioned at this point. The first is an area of land known as 'Burnt Cumberworth' which lies to the North of High Flatts, behind the Sovereign Public House. This area is in danger of being lost for good unless the quarrying activities which border it are discontinued. Remains of a floor, and a number of ridges in the ground were noted by Henry Moorhouse, though today the ridges are not so clear, but the settlement is thought to be of British Celtic origin. The second is the hillfort at Almondbury. First occupied by Neolithic man, it could have connections with the High Flatts activity at this time. Later the site was abandoned, until, as at High Flatts, it was refortified during the Iron Age, circa 590 BC. Though it is possible that there were links with High Flatts, it is certain that the two sites were well known to each other.

Naturally, far more archaeological evidence lies buried under today's modern villages and field systems, but these latter two sites do at least suspend the feeling of isolation created whilst considering the settlement at High Flatts as a single unit.

10

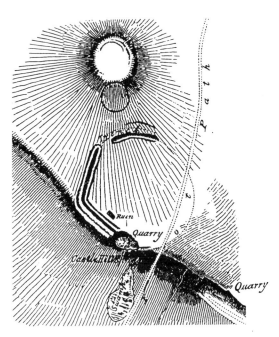

Henry Moorhouses plan of the High Flatts Castle Hill site.

Britain at the time of the Roman conquest was populated by a number of tribal groups, each controlling a significant area of land, minting their own coins and regularly warring against each other. When Emperor Claudius ordered the second invasion of Brittania in AD 43 (the first by Julius Caesar had broken neither the country or its people) the tribes either made alliances with the Romans, and became 'client Kingdoms' or fought with great hostility.

Most of us have heard of Boadicea (or Boudicca as she should be called) of the Iceni tribe, from East Anglia. After the death of her husband Boudicca was flogged and her daughters raped by the Romans. Her incredible revolt left thousands dead until she herself saw her forces annihilated and so took a lethal dose of poison.

Aulus Plautius arrived from Rome with 50,000 men in AD43. The south of Briton, Wales and East Anglia were conquered under the generalship of Vespasian, and finally, by AD74 Cerialis (a future Governor of Briton) had subdued the Brigantes, although there were several uprisings, indeed the Brigantes continued to resist for some time. Cerialis continued North towards the lands of the Cruithne or Picts. Picts was the name ascribed to these people by the Romans - it meant 'painted men'.

As a result of internal disputes and to defend their northern dominions the Emperor Hadrian built in 122AD his great wall which was completed in 130AD, 73 miles long stretching from the Tyne to the Solway Firth it was designed to separate the tribes of the Selgovae and Novantae of the central lowlands from the Brigantes of Yorkshire. A further turf wall, known as the Antonine wall was constructed later a few miles to the north but was abandoned in 165AD following new incursions by the Brigantes.

The Romans left Britain in AD 410 after Emperor Honorius had proclaimed, that, 'the British province should henceforth fend for itself', the legions left, abandoning the country to take up positions in other provinces as the Empire began to creek under the weight of invasions against it. They left behind them a country of cultural and architectural wealth and a road system which is still in use today, indeed some aspects of their civilisation continued after their withdrawal but these quickly collapsed during the fifth century.

It has been suggested that a Roman camp was set up on the abandoned settlement at High Flatts but there is no evidence for this whatsoever and is probably a lame attempt at describing the site for entry into the trade directories of the nineteenth century.

THE DARK AGES

This period so named because of the scarcity of written historical evidence is gradually being re-evaluated due to the efforts of archaeologists. The British monk Gildas, the Venerable Bede and the Saxon Chronicle are three of the main written resources but as far as Denby is concerned there are few specifics.

Generally, after the departure of the legions the country reverted back to its original tribal identities. There was much warfare as petty Kings struggled for supremacy. Then in the late 4th and early 5th centuries the Germanic tribes began to arrive. They were first employed as mercenaries, by the Romans and later by British Kings, such as Vortigern, who used them in his wars against the Scotti (from Ireland) and the Picts in the North. These mercenaries were settled in the south east, according to legend the first to arrive were the brothers Hengist and Horsa.

Gradually more tribes arrived, Jutes, Angles and Saxons who began to settle and then conquer. The Angles from the northern part of the Danish peninsula took over lands which were to become Northumbria, and consequently the area included the land that was to become Denby. This wasn't a blanket settlement, we know from archaeological evidence that Saxons were also involved, though seemingly in fewer numbers than elsewhere.

Aided by internal strife between the Britons, they swept North and West meeting only meek resistance. Various fightbacks did take place, including the famous battle of Badon Hill (possibly King Arthur), which gave the Britons, according to Gildas, 50 years or so of peace, but the writing was on the wall and the Anglo Saxons (as they became known) were here to stay. In many cases they settled, farmed, and inter-married with the native Celts, at least those that weren't pushed back into what is now Wales (Welsh in Anglo Saxon means foreigner) and so the Britons were finally defeated and the English took over. Examples of how far they spread can be seen in local place names :

CALTORNE (Cawthorne), CHIZEBURG (Kexborough), and CUMBER (Cumberworth) are all Celtic.
SHEPLEY, SHELLEY, CLAYTON, BRETTON, and EMLEY are all Saxon. Words ending
in ..'TON indicate a homestead or enclosure, words ending in .. LEY (LEA) indicate a meadow.

Great internal Kingdoms grew such as Mercia, Wessex, East Anglia, Kent and the one to which Denby belonged NORTHUMBRIA. The Northumbrian lands covered much of the north of England, the Kingdom being formed by Ethelfrith in the early 7th century consisting of the smaller kingdoms of Bernicia, Deira and the one to which Denby was to belong, Elmet. Elmet was established after the withdrawal of the Romans and was located in the foothills of the Pennines, it wasn't until the reign of Edwin, first of the 7th century Northumbrian Bretwaldas (Overall rulers of England) that it was incorporated into this larger territory, around 630AD.

Internal strife between the ruling dynasties in England became its undoing as towards the end of the 8th century a new threat emerged from the Scandinavian coasts.

THE VIKINGS

Extract from the Anglo Saxon Chronicle.....

AD 793 This year came dreadful fore-warnings over the land of the Northumbrians, terrifying the people most woefully : these were immense sheets of light rushing through the air, and whirlwinds and fiery dragons flying across the firmament. These tremendous tokens were soon followed by a great famine; and not long after on the sixth day before the ides of January in the same year, the harrowing inroads of heathen men made lamentable havoc in the Church of God in Holy Island, by rapine and slaughter.

The extract refers to the Viking attack on Lindisfarne. The word 'Viking' means sea-raider or sea-pirate and doesn't differentiate between Norse and Danish cultures. As with the raid on Lindisfarne, they at first came for 'plunder and glory' but these raids became more significant from the 830's and culminated in their conquest of much of the country during the decade, 865-875 AD.

Devotees of the Kirk Douglas film, 'The Vikings' will remember that Ernest Borgnine played the part of the Viking chief, Ragnar and that he died in a pit of wolves. It may come as a surprise to learn that Ragnar Lothbrok, on whom the character was based was a real historical character, though according to legend he didn't die at the hand of the Northumbrian King, Aelle, but in Ireland, in a pit of snakes! Ragnar was a Danish warrior and it was two of his sons that became co-leaders in the 'Great Army' formed in 865, Ivar the Boneless and Halfdan Ragnarsson. One by one the great English Kingdoms fell, Mercia, East Anglia, Kent and Northumbria, who due to initial civil chaos fell easy prey to these fearless warriors. Eofforwic was taken in 866 and held in 867 after an Anglian counteroffensive, the city being renamed Jorvik, now York. The Northumbrian King, Aelle was subjected by Ivar to the terrible Viking 'blood eagle'. He was tied to a stake and had his ribs and lungs torn from his body and spread out like the wings of an eagle whilst still alive. This barbaric end to Aelle probably served as a ritualistic sacrifice to the Danish God - Odin (Norse - Woden).

Only Wessex remained unconquered, resisting Viking attacks and paying 'Danegeld' to buy peace, from time to time. It was under the leadership of Alfred the Great that the Kingdom was finally rescued. The Viking chieftain, Guthrum had penetrated deep into the heart of the Kingdom, but against the odds was defeated by Alfred at Eddington in 875. Guthrum was baptised and converted to Christianity. The country remained split, and systems of law and government developed along cultural lines. Broadly speaking, Anglo Saxon in the West and South, Danish in the North and East, this Danish area later developed the title the 'Danelaw'.

Ivar the Boneless died in 873, leaving his brother Halfdan as King of Jorvik. Halfdan abandoned the conquest of Wessex for pursuits elsewhere, notably in Ireland. By 876 his fighting men must have been around 40 years old, by Medieval standards too old and as was a Kings duty Halfdan was obliged to grant gifts to them in return for their loyal service, a little like the retirement presents of today:

Extract from the Saxon Chronicle:
AD 876 : 'And in this year Halfdan apportioned the land of the Northumbrians and from that time they (the Danes) continued ploughing and tilling them'.

Halfdan wasn't for settling, ultimately entering Valhalla in battle whilst many of his men lived out the rest of their lives working on the farmsteads that he had granted to them. It is possible that Denby was created at this time, although Scandinavian settlement in the area continued for over another century. As the name suggests Denebi was the farmstead of the Danes and it could be that its original occupants were former members of Halfdan's army. It is now impossible to suggest where the original site of the settlement in Denby was. Many successful farmsteads became Medieval villages and now both lie buried under their modern counterparts. I would speculate that the medieval pot (examined later) dated 1350-1400 discovered in the field above the modern day village green suggests occupation in this area 600 years ago. If the latter theory is correct then the Danish farmstead could not have been far away.

The farmstead itself was probably enclosed amidst an associated field system. Buildings would have included a long house (living quarters) and perhaps a bakery, a grindstone, an oven, a simple smithy, or indeed any variation thereof.

So by now the country was populated by many diverse peoples, Saxons, Angles, Friesans, Jutes, Danes, Celts, Scotti, Picts, Irish, Roman, Norse and the original Britons, all originally practising differing ways of life and religion - though initially all were predominantly pagan. Now living alongside each other, embracing Christianity, inter-marrying and creating one unique new culture - the English.

13

THE DOMESDAY BOOK

William the Conquerors victory over Harold Godwinson at the battle of Hastings in 1066 is history known to every schoolchild, though it is unlikely that Harold died from an arrow wound to his eye. William brought about an incredible transformation in English society, and also left the country with its foremost literary evidence of the period the Domesday Book, dating from 1086.

Extract from the Saxon Chronicle

AD 1085 : *Then at midwinter was the king at Gloucester with his council, and held there his court five days. And afterwards the Archbishop and clergy had a synod three days.....*

After this had the King a large meeting, and very deep consultation with his council, about this land; how it was occupied, and by what sort of men. Then sent he his men over all England into each shire; commissioning them to find out "how many hundreds (wapentakes) of hides were in the shire, what land the King himself had, and what stock upon the land; or, what dues he ought to have by the year from the shire." Also he commissioned them to record in writing, "How much land his Archbishops had, and his diocesan bishops and his Abbots, and his Earls;" and though I may be prolix and tedious, "what or how much, each man had, who was an occupier in England, either in land or in stock, and how much money it were worth." So very narrowly indeed did he commission them to trace it out, that there was not one single hide, nor a yard of land, nay, moreover (it is shameful to tell, though he thought it no shame to do it), not even an ox, nor a cow, nor a swine was there left, that was not set down in his writ. And all the recorded particulars were afterwards brought to him.

The country was most likely divided into areas, perhaps 8 or 9 and a group of William's men would be responsible for each. These areas were then divided into hundreds, or in lands previously subject to the Danelaw, wapentakes. The word Wapentake is of Scandinavian origin and refers to the voting done at gatherings by the brandishing of weapons. Men from each village were called to their local court to answer the Kings questions. Denby was included in the Staincross wapentake and the following information was recorded :

In (Upper and Lower) Denby, Eadwulf and Godric had 3 carucates of land taxable where 1½ ploughs are possible. Now Alric has (them) from Ilbert. There, woodland pasture, 1 league long and 1 wide. Value before 1066, 10s; now 6s. A cow pasture is there.'

The above translation comes from the Phillimore edition of the Domesday Book, 1986. A slight variation on this comes from Fred Lawton's 'Historical Notes on Skelmanthorpe and District' reprinted 1986:

2, manors. In Denebi, Edulf and Godric had three carucates of land to be taxed, where there may be one plough and a half. Alric now has of Ilbert. Wood pasture one mile long and one broad. Value in King Edward's time 10s now 6s. There is waste ground.

So what can we learn from this? Lawton mentions the melancholy phrase 'there is waste ground' which refers to the problems William the Conqueror had in subduing his northern subjects. Frequent rebellions and attacks on the city of York finally tried his patience and he rode to what became known as the 'Harrying of the North' in the winter of 1069/70. It took him less than two years to devastate Northumbria, his men killing the people and livestock alike and burning all buildings and tools. The bulk of the population either died or became refugees, hence the reduction of the land values at the time of writing of the Domesday Book.

Although the statement is used many times in the Phillimore edition it is conspicuous by its absence from the entry for Denby. Lawton has, conversely, omitted one of the most interesting features :

'Ibi est vaccaria' - 'there is a cow pasture' or 'there is a cattle house'. This statement was unique to Denby in the whole Yorkshire survey, though there would surely have been others. What was a cattle house?, it seems best to suggest that this was a place where cattle were kept and bred, for resale. It is also very interesting to note that the remains of the hill settlement at High Flatts (which would have been more significant at this time) have been linked with the vaccaria. It is possible that the two were one and the same and that the settlement was being re-used to good effect. The 'Victoria County History' suggests as much and the thought has not been lost on the 'West Yorkshire Archaeology Service'. In effect we shall never know for sure and to make this assumption without further evidence would be foolish.

Edulf or Eadwulf and Godric are testament to the fact that agricultural activity had been considerable before the conquest. A carucate was the amount of land that could be ploughed by an eight ox plough team and this was composed of bovates, which was the amount of land that could be ploughed by one ox in a year, thus, eight bovates to a carucate. Bovates were also known as Oxgangs. The detail 'where 1½ ploughs are possible' refers to the total equipment at the farmers disposal, which when assembled became a plough.

Altough next to nothing is known of Edulf or Eadwulf and Godric the survey of 1086 does give an indication that Godric was the senior partner. When the lands apportioned to Ilbert de Lacy by the King were re-apportioned to tennants many of the original landlords dissappear. Siward, Halfdan, Thorbjorn and Alsige alongside Eadwulf and Godric are dispossessed by the time of the survey. Names such as Gammall, Sveinn, Arnbjorn, Asulfr and Alric appear, people noted before the conquest in a state of elevation after it. Perhaps the former mentioned were involved in resistance against the Normans either during the battles of 1066 or fighting against King William during the 'Harrying of the North'. Their deaths would explain their absence from their lands noted in the survey, though they could have died of old age.

Godric of Denby is almost certainly the same Godric that held lands at Kexborough and had his Hall at Notton, North of Royston, between Wakefield and Barnsley. Noting that a vaccary was sited at Denby it would appear that he and Eadwulf were cattle farmers, though Godric may have had other interests on his lands at Kexborough and perhaps around Notton. After the Conquest Alric inherited his lands at Denby and Sveinn (not to be confussed with the son of Alric) those at Kexborough. Notton was held directly by Ilbert de Lacy. Eadwulf is not mentioned after the Conquest at all and seems to have only held land at Denby.

It would seem unlikely that the landlords names during Edward the Confessors time would be important twenty years later and though it is a more heroic notion to have these men dieing resisting the Normans it is just as probable that they were merely dispossessed in favour of more amenable tennants to the Normans.

Alric or Ailric was a large landholder in the time of Edward the Confessor, (1042-1066), Birchworth, Hoyland, Silkstone, Cumberworth, Skelmanthorpe, Penistone and Cawthorne- (where he is believed to have lived) were all in his possession. The antiquarian, John Leland notes in his itinerary, written during the 1530's and 40's, that a Richard Aschenald was the father of Aelric (Alric) and that his grandson was Swane. Swane's son was Adam and he had two daughters who were married to Geoffrey Neville and Thomas Burge. Before the conquest, Aschenald held lands at Pontefract, which subsequently passed to Ilbert De Lacy who when granted his lands by William the Conqueror was obliged to parcel them out to tenants, evidently Alric had caused little trouble to the Normans and so received grants of land, many of which he had held previously : Cawthorne, Silkstone, Hoyland, Clayton, Penistone and now DENBY.

He was succeeded by his son, Sveinn who made various donations to Pontefract Priory. Sveinn also received an extensive Lordship in Cumberland from Henry I (1101-1135) and his sons, Adam and Henry also held lands in Cumberland and Lancashire. Adam founded Monk Bretton Priory around 1156.

Ilbert De Lacy arrived in the Conquerors vanguard, and after helping to subdue the English was given 164 manors in the counties of York, Nottingham and Lincoln. These lands were confirmed to him in the tenth year of William's reign, 1076.

He was probably a vassal of Odo of Bayeux from whom he held moderate fees in Lincolnshire and the south midlands. He and his brother, Walter, who was an important Lord in the Welsh marches, were in the second rank of Norman Lords, owing their rank to their military skill. Ilbert's position was further advanced when he was granted the Honour of Pontefract, where he founded the Collegiate Chapel of St. Clement within Pontefract castle.

He was succeeded by his son, Robert (circa 1095), and he in turn by his son, Ilbert. The family continued to add to its possessions and were the forbears of the Earls of Lincoln.

The De Lacy lineage, according to Fred Lawton, continued thus:

Ilbert De Lacy	died early 12th century.
Robert De Lacy	son of above.
Ilbert De Lacy	son of above.
Henry De Lacy	brother of above Ilbert.
Robert De Lacy	son of above, died 1198.
Albreda Ligours	half sister to above Robert, married Richard Lord of Halton. Their son, John, assumed the name, De Lacy.
John De Lacy	see above.
Roger De Lacy	son of John.
John De Lacy	son of Roger, Earl of Lincoln, died 1240.
Edmund De Lacy	son of John.
HENRY DE LACY	son of Edmund, see below.
Alice De Lacy	only daughter and sole heiress.

It is a remarkable coincidence that Denby in Yorkshire is connected with Denbigh in Clwyd, North Wales, the link being the second Henry De Lacy, mentioned above.

Henry was the campaign commander of King Edward I's armies in Wales. He also owned Pontefract Castle, founded by his illustrious forbear, the first Ilbert. During the latter part of October 1282, the King and De Lacy were at Denbigh, planning new fortifications. De Lacy was left in charge of these after the Kings departure. The site chosen was an impressive outcrop of rock in the Vale of Clwyd, the name Denbigh actually incorporating the Welsh word 'Dinas', meaning a rocky fortress. Today the castle is all too frequently overshadowed by its neighbours at Conwy, Caernarvon, Harlech and Beaumaris, but its remains still stand as a testament to its builders over 700 years ago.

Henry De Lacy's elder son, Edmund is said to have fallen to his death in the well at Denbigh castle in 1308. His younger son, John, died when he fell from the battlements at Pontefract castle whilst chasing a ball. This meant that it was his only daughter, Alice who inherited from Henry. Alice married Thomas, Earl of Lancaster, the rebel who fought against King Edward II at Boroughbridge in 1322 and was beheaded after his defeat. It is also interesting to note that one of the followers of the Earl was a Robert Hood of Wakefield. Although not the originator of the legend he certainly contributed significantly to the tales about Robin Hood, but we must now return to the development of Denby.

Arriving with the Conqueror, along with the Lacy's were the families of Bosville and Burdet, although initially neither had connections with Denby both were to play a major role in the formation and development of the village which we will examine in the next chapter.

EARLY SUBINFEUDATION

The story of Denby and its subsequent growth is closely intertwined with the Lords of the Manor. The Landholders on whose property all others dwelt, be they Serf, Labourer or Yeoman.

The Lords of the Manor wielded absolute authority over the lives of the peasants that farmed their lands. The lowest class of peasants were the serfs, who were not even paid for their work and were only able to keep their homes by paying their Lord with a large portion of their yearly produce. The next class up were the labourers and small tradesmen, unlike the serfs, who lived on the farmland, these people lived in villages and paid both rent to their Lord and tax to the crown. Villages were small houses built of timber and mudbrick, with shutters to cover the windows. Food was basic and meat a luxury item. In these villages, some homes were larger and more permanently built, these belonged to the emerging middle class, the Yeoman, who were generally, more highly paid employees of the estate. Upon this background we will now examine the Lords of Denby, the original instigators of today's modern village.

It was the Heralds of Elizabeth I who were first responsible for creating a pedigree,(by which they were able to authenticate the Coat of Arms of the family of Burdet), for the early Lords of Denby.

Heralds, originally began as announcers and organisers of tournaments, they were also used as diplomats, but during the 16th century they gained formal jurisdiction over the granting and definition of coats of arms. They made frequent visitations to investigate and authenticate the lineage and right to bear arms of families such as the Burdet's, and left us the following pedigree:

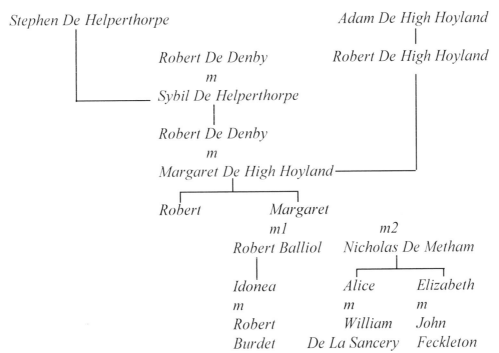

This pedigree, although a foundation, gives us very little concerning the early De Denby family, and so we will regress a little to try and flesh out these early Lords.

Rev. Joseph Hunter in his 'South Yorkshire Vol. II' supplies us with the following information which he discovered, regarding the De Denby family:

1) Mathew De Denby   (found in the pipe rolls of Henry II 1154-89)

2) John De Denby   (son of Adam De Denby. John and his wife Christian gave the Monks of

Bretton 3 acres of land in Denby at a place called Ebriches, by deed, with free common right through the whole township).

3) William De Denby   (found in the rolls of the Lords of Midhope, who married Sarah, daughter of Sir Alexander Venavre, who had an elder son who was Lord of Denby and Okynthorpe) (NB: Hunter believed that the author of these rolls con sidered that the Lords of Barmby were of the same stock as the De Denby's).

4) Robert De Denby   (son of Robert De Denby, found in a rent agreement in Penistone as a witness in 1306).

5) William De Denby   (along with his son, Robert were also witnesses to a deed relating to the land rights of the De Gunthwaite's).

Further research, by Dr. David Hey, has revealed an,

6) Agnes De Denby   (recorded in the Wakefield Court Rolls of 1297 as paying 6d for licence to take 3 acres of land in the west field at Upperthong).

Another historical figure recorded at this time as Lord of Denby, was William Fitz Osbert. He made a grant to the Monks of Byland Abbey, soon after 1177, empowering then to extend their mining operations for their iron industry in the village. The original grant was made to the monks by the Lord of Bretton, Sveinn, the activity being concentrated around what is now Papist Hall Farm. This grant contributed to the feud between the monks of Byland and their Rievaulx counterparts who were jealous of their neighbours accumulating wealth.

The present day remains of Byland Abbey, the monks of which, mined on lands granted to them in Denby in the 12th Century.

Until recently this confused and rather sparten picture was all that was known of these ancient Lords, but a series of previously unused documents from the John Goodchild collection in Wakefield has now enabled a fuller picture to be drawn.

A deed dated between 1217 and 1265, has Nicholas Burdet transferring his lands in Skelmanthorpe to his brother Robert. Possibly the same Robert, mentioned in the pedigree drawn by the heralds. The document also states that the lands were originally given by his Uncle, William De Denby to his mother

Agnes. This must surely be the same Agnes alive in 1297 as discussed above. The document was witnessed amongst others by a John Burdet.

A further grant drawn up at the same time has Almaricus Burdet transferring his land to Thomas De Denby, land which Thomas's father, William, once gave to Agnes his daughter, land which was originally given as a dowry to his wife Cecilia when she married William De Denby, by Adam de Hoyland. The land was in Skelmanthorpe and the document goes on to say that Almaricus Burdet had held it after the death of his wife, Agnes.

This document, now takes the earliest known evidence of occupation by the Burdet family back another generation, and also shows that inter family marriage could occur generation after generation. Almaricus Burdet married Agnes De Denby and Robert Burdet (Almaricus's son) married Idonea De Denby.

A further document dated 24th September 1304 concerns Richard Burdet of Randde, Knight, appointing Jon de la Grange, with power of attorney.

The document concludes :

"This is a notice by me William, son of Henry, son of Simon, to Robert Burdeth my brother in accordance with the charter which he had from me"

This document suggests that there could have been two Robert Burdet's living as contemporaries, the document is included in the collection on Denby and relates to land in Skelmanthorpe but could refer to a later Robert Burdet.

The situation remains complicated and open to varying interpretation, the genealogical table overleaf is based on what I have been able to re-construct from all the available evidence and should help to simplify matters somewhat.

IN CONCLUSION:

1) The earliest mention of the family of De Denby (of Denby) occurs with the names of Mathew and Adam De Denby, probably contemporary with Adam Fitz Svienn, grandson of Alric mentioned in the Domesday Book, these two were certainly alive and active during the period 1154 - 1189.

2) Adam de (High) Hoyland seems to have passed on his lands and estates to his siblings, which in turn were married into the De Denby family, during the period 1220-1260.

3) It is possible that William De Denby and Robert De Denby II who married, respectively; Cecilia De Hoyland and Margaret De Hoyland were brothers, they must have been at the very least, cousins.

4) Nicholas and Richard Burdet are both described as knights of Randde, Nicholas names his brother, Robert and his mother Agnes. The document is dated around 1260, and is in the Denby collection.

5) In 1304 William Burdet names his father Henry and his grandfather, Simon, and names HIS brother, Robert.

6) Almaricus Burdet was the husband of Agnes De Denby and they had a son named, Robert. Agnes's father was William De Denby and her brother Thomas De Denby. Agnes died before Almaricus, yet she was alive in 1297.

7)   According to the Heralds, Robert De Denby III died without issue and so the Lordship of Denby passed to Margaret, his sister who was married to Robert Balliol. Almaricus Burdet and Agnes were contemporary with Margaret, around 1300.

8)   Inter marriage between De Denby and Burdet was not unusual and there are at least two positive examples of this in Almaricus Burdet and Agnes De Denby and their son Robert Burdet and Idonea Balliol.

9)   The evidence for even earlier settlement by the Burdet family is compelling, it could perhaps even be argued that the two families started out one and the same and that the De Denby's were the first members of the family to settle in Denby and took the name of the village for their own before being followed by more illustrious members of the family from such places as Rand(de) and Lowesby.

Genealogical Table Showing Descent of De Denby & Burdet

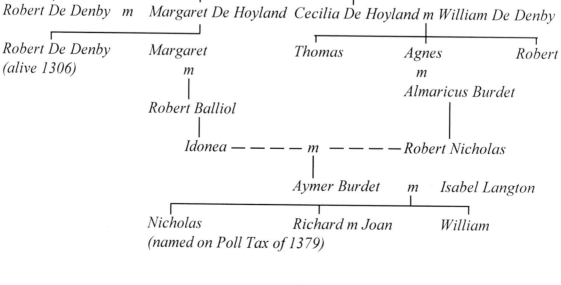

10) Finally, the Hoyland and Denby estates which had been passed down through the eldest male line of descent finally belonged to the Burdet family with the marriage of Robert Burdet to Idonea Balliol.

THE BALLIOL'S

Robert (de) Balliol shares the same surname as the John and Edward who in turn became Kings of the Scots. John Balliol (1250-1313) was King from 1292-96 until he surrendered his throne to Edward I. His successor, Robert Bruce went on to crush the English at Bannockburn in 1314 and then signed a truce with King Edward II. He died of leprosy in 1329 leaving his five year old son as King. Internal strife enabled Edward Balliol (John's son) to become King in 1332, but his hold on the crown was very much dependent on English arms. He was eventually to surrender the Scottish crown to Edward III in 1356, he died in 1364.

It is quite possible that Robert Balliol who married Margaret De Denby was of the same strain as these two Kings and that the Burdet family married into Royal blood (perhaps a thought not lost on Almaricus Burdet). According to 'Hunter' there were plaster work coats of arms inside the old 'Birthwaite Hall' (discussed later), these coats of arms depicted the families which had married into the Burdet lineage over the years, and according to 'Hunter' the orle of the Balliol's was, a favourite bearing of the Burdet's, and appeared upon the seal of the first Sir Francis. Hunter also goes-on to suggest that the orle might be seen carved in stone on the tower of the church of Darton. If Robert Balliol was a member of this Royal family and the evidence would appear to suggest as much then he could have been either a brother or cousin to John Balliol, rather than Edward who seems to have been much younger.

A grant survives, dated between 1304 and 1309 made out by Robert Burdet, It states that he and Nicholas de Wortelaye had granted the manors of Denby and Heghholand (High Hoyland) to Robert de Balliol and Margaret his wife in the Kings court by a fine levied between them. This meant that Robert Balliol and Margaret were to hold the manors for life after which they should pass to their daughter, Idonea and her husband Robert Burdet, with a further clause stating that should this be impossible then the heirs of Margaret should inherit. The grant continues :

' Robert Burdet grants that by reason of the cost of repairing or ruin of the houses, gardens, woods, tenantry or anything else made by Robert de Balliol or Margaret within the said manors the grant will not oppress them by writ or waste or any other plea, wishing and granting for himself and his heirs that Robert de Balliol and Margaret may approve as much in wastes, marl pits (manure), turbaries (a place where peat is dug) and mines as exel."

The grant appears to show that Robert Burdet was the Lord of the manor of Denby at this time. It is possible that Agnes de Denby who married Almaricus Burdet brought to the union the manors of Denby and Hoyland and that Almaricus inherited after her demise. If this is the case then it would appear that the heralds of Elizabeth I got it wrong, and although the genealogy may be correct the descent of the Denby estate did not involve the De Denby's that they discovered. It should also be remembered that the Burdet's may not have lived in the village at this time and so appropriating their lands to tenants, particularly, members of their family was the natural option.

NB: I was informed that the tomb of Lady Idonea was in Beverley Minster. It seems that this is incorrect. Although the name is uncommon, the Idonea at Beverley is buried in the Percy family vault and was the wife of a gentleman of that family. Further research would be required to find out if Robert Burdet died young and if Idonea remarried. It is possible as the Percy lineage does include a number of different Balliol's, but the Idonea at Beverley appears to have been living far too late to correspond with the Lady of Denby.

ORIGIN OF BURDET

The ancestral home of the Burdet's was in Normandy and the name in its earliest form was written Burdet, Bordet or Bowdett. Although other variations were possible as we have seen i.e.Burdeth. Its origin is uncertain. In 1862 the 'Societe De Archaeologie of France' erected a plate in the church of Dives not far from Deauville in Normandy to commemorate the companions of the conqueror some 450 in number. Among these names are Hugo Boordet, Robert Burdet, and Ernis De Boron. In return for his services to the conquest Hugo Burdet was given lands in Leicestershire, the greater part of his property being at Lowesby and it was here that the family established itself, Hugo becoming lord of Lowesby. Later the Burdet's acquired more and more property, particularly around the area where Leics.,Derbys., and Warwickshire join, east of Tamworth. In 1159 William Burdet, great grandson of Hugo founded Ancote Priory in Warwickshire, to expiate the rash killing of his wife whom a false steward had accused of infidelity during Burdet's absence in the Holy Land during a crusade.

NB: In its earlier form Burdet was spelt with only one T, later records, from around the late 17th century begin using a further T, leaving us with the spelling we have today, Burdett. It should be remembered that it was up to the individual scribe as to how to spell the name on official records and so for the purposes of this book I have tried, as far as possible to use whichever form was originally recorded.

THE GUNTHWAITE'S & BOSVILLE'S

It would be useful at this point to examine the early Lords of Gunthwaite and consider the descent of these powerful neighbours of the De Denby's and Burdet's.

A family called De Byrton from Kirkburton held these lands originally before they passed through an heiress to the Darcy family. In 1281 John de Rodes de Gunnildthwayt made a quitclaim to his Lord, Henry de Byrton, regarding all waste land from the Gunthwaite estate, this deed was interestingly enough witnessed by John, son of Alan de Denby, amongst others.

A charter drawn up during the time of Edward III (1327-1377) has Henry Darcy of London granting John Gonildthwaite lands in Gunthwaite and also the water mill thereby elevating the Gunthwaite's to a landowning position instead of the tenants they had previously been under the De Byrton's and Darcy's. This grant gave John and his wife Christiana the manors for their lifetime, but on their deaths it was to pass to Thomas Bosville of Ardsley (east of Barnsley) and his heirs. The document was dated Sunday October 20th 1359 and was witnessed by John De Dronsfield, John De Stainton and AYMER BURDET. In 1374, John de Gunthwaite was dead and his wife released the manor to Thomas Bosville. It seems that the reason for the Bosville inheritance was that John and Christiana's daughter, Alice, was the wife of Thomas of Ardsley, though there is no documentary proof of this. Thus the Bosville's took over at Gunthwaite.

The Bosville's were, like the Burdet's, part of the conquerors vanguard. They originated from the place in Normandy, Bosville, 'Bos' meaning Ox and 'ville' meaning town. Sir Martin Bosville was treasurer for William the Conquerors army and later also for William Rufus. He died in 1092 having had three sons,. William, John and Ellias. It was from John that Thomas Bosville of Ardsley was descended.

THE BURDET EXPANSION

As we have already noted, the manors of Denby and Hoyland were united during the mid 13th century and that they fell into the hands of the Burdet's around 1300-1315. We will now follow the family and the village of Denby up until the two manors were separated, and when the family was split into two very distinct branches. The genealogical chart on the opposite page will help this process.

The first Aymer (possibly short for Almaricus) appears to have died at a relatively young age, for his wife, Isabel, remarried afterwards to Ralph Hyde. He was certainly alive and active in 1341 when he and

John de Gunthwaite witnessed a charter at Penistone, and of course we have already seen that he was a witness to the grant which gave the aforementioned John his manor at Gunthwaite in 1359, after which the records are silent, presumably he died soon after.

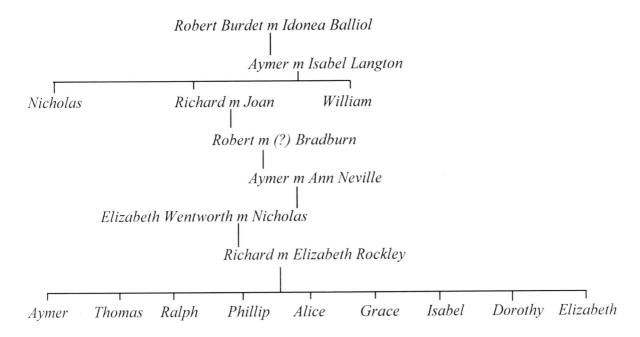

THE POLL TAX OF 1379

The next record of the Burdet's and one which for the first time gives us the names of the ordinary villagers of Denby is the Poll Tax. This was levied in the reign of Richard II (1367-1400) and was, as now, unpopular with the public. A Kent man, named Wat Tyler organised a revolt only two years later in 1381, leading peasants against landowners airing grievances about the Poll Tax and the feudal system in general. He led his followers into London where he presented a petition to a young King Richard. As Tyler and the King drew nearer the Mayor of London, in the belief that Tyler was about to do the King harm, slew him with his sword. To appease the angry crowd the King offered to take Tyler's place and lead the rebels, he then pardoned them all. With Tyler dead and the crowd disbursed it took the government only a few days to revoke these pardons.

Denby appears in the Staincross section of the returns as can be seen from the printed version, dated 1882.

It should be noted that the Lord of the Manor, Nicholas Burdet appears with his brother William, and either a servant or daughter, Diot. The De Denby's are also still very much in evidence and the Robinson and Marshall families make their first appearance. John Marshall and John De Denby were both smiths and are the only two with a trade after their names.

The total amount to be collected from Denby was 11s 8d, the following villages make an interesting comparison :

CLAYTON	3s 8d	PENISTONE	5s 2d
INGBIRCHWORTH	3s 2d	GUNTHWAITE	4s 6d
CUMBERWORTH	5s 6d	HIGH HOYLAND	3s 6d
HOYLANDSWAINE	6s 8d	KEXBOROUGH	6s 2d

The highest local amount came from Cawthorne with 47s 2d, followed by Barnsley with, 33s 8d.

The following is my rough translation of the tax :

THE DENBY POLL TAX ROLL - 1379

Villata De Denby		*Village of Denby*	
Nicolaus Burdet,ffrankeleyn	xl.d	Nicholas Burdet, freeholder	40d
Willelmus,frater,ejus	iiii.d	William Burdet, brother	4d
Diot,famula,ejus	iiii.d	Diot, daughter of above	4d
Willelmus Elkoc	iiii.d	William Elcock.	4d
Thomas Dey Alicia vx-ejus	iiii.d	Thomas Day & Alice his wife	4d
Robertus Bromele vx	iiii.d	Robert Bromley & his wife	4d
Johanna Horn	iiii.d	Joanna Horn	4d
Johannes, Marschall Alicia vx smyth	vi.d	John Marshall & Alicia, wife Smith	6d
Johannes,fillius,ejus	iiii.d	John, son of above	4d
Alicia,famula,ejus	iiii.d	Alicia daughter of above	4d
Johannes Skalter & vx ejus	iiii.d	John Skalter & his wife	4d
Johannes Buring & vx ejus	iiii.d	John Buring & his wife	4d
Ricardus de Denby & vx	iiii.d	Richard de Denby & his wife	4d
Johannes Robynson & vx	iiii.d	John Robinson & his wife	4d
Thomas Pek & vx ejus	iiii.d	Thomas Pek & his wife	4d
Johannes Dicson & vx	iiii.d	John Dixon & his wife	4d
Johannes de Denby & vx smyth	vi.d	John de Denby & his wife Smith	6d
Ricardus de Denby	iiii.d	Richard de Denby	4d
Simon Horn	iiii.d	Simon Horn	4d
Elena,filia ejus	iiii.d	Elena daughter of above	4d
Johannes Dicson minor & vx	iiii.d	John Dixon minor&wife	4d
Johannes filius Johannis	iiii.d	John son of John	4d
Ricardus de Haytfield vx	iiii.d	Richard de Hatfield & wife	4d
Radulphus de Denby vx	iiii.d	Radulphus de Denby & wife	4d
Robertus Elkoc & vx ejus	iiii.d	Robert Elkoc & wife	4d
Summa xjs.	viii.d	Total	11s 8d

From the latter we know that Nicholas Burdet had inherited from Aymer by 1379 and he was still alive in 1402 when he is recorded as a witness to a transfer of ownership of Gunthwaite Hall. Nicholas died before 1408 without an heir and so the manor passed to his brother Richard.

In 1408 a land grant was drawn up by Richard Burdet to William Scott, Vicar of Dewsbury, John de Manygham of Ardeslawe, William de Maltby and John Walker of Mirfield, chaplain. It gave them all his manors in Denby and High Hoyland and all his land in Yorkshire, document dated 6 December 1408. This was followed by a quitclaim made by William Scott and John de Manyngham to William de Maltby and John Walker, leaving them to pass the lands back to Richard Burdet and his wife Joan later in the year, with a proviso that if Richard should die without an heir the properties should pass to the Lord of Wortley.

Richard and Joan did produce an heir, Robert who married a daughter of (?)Bradburn. Robert witnessed a deed in 1429 and could possibly be the Robert Burdet, referred to by Hunter, as being buried at Penistone church in 1451, unfortunately the early records of the church have not survived to prove this.

His son Aymer II, inherited his fathers estates and was living in 1456 when he was a witness to a deed, his life continued at least until the reign of Edward IV (1461-1483). He married Ann Neville, daughter of Sir Thomas Neville of Liversedge and had a son and heir, Nicholas II. In 1508, Nicholas made a quitclaim to Richard Beaumont of Whitley with regard to land rights at Shepley. He was married to Elizabeth Wentworth, the daughter of Richard Wentworth of the powerful Bretton Lords. It appears that Aymer II had granted his lands in Denby, Hoyland, Barnsley, Netherbretton, Mapilwell, Clayton, Darton, Kexborough and Keresforth to the Normanville family. Nicholas II had died by 1522, by which time he had been succeeded by his son Richard II.

A document dated 12th May 1522 has Robert Normanville, son of Ralph granting the above lands back to Richard with all their, "messuages, rights and appurtenances".

We have concentrated solely on the Lords of the Manor and their heirs in the Burdet family, but it should be remembered that there were many more siblings throughout these generations, and though they did not have the opportunity to accede to the title 'Lord of the Manor', they did come from a wealthy background and achieved positions of authority and respect in other areas, such as the John Burdet who became Vicar of Cumberworth in 1365 after being presented by John de Dronsfield.

We have a detail of a Denby yeoman in the time of Richard Burdet II named William Marshall. He received a payment of rent from William Blackburn of Huddersfield to the value of 5 shillings. He granted it to Richard and others who decided that it should be used for the Priest of the Chantry Chapel of St John the Baptist in Penistone who would receive 4s 11d, leaving the one remaining penny to be paid to William Marshall and his heirs.

Richard Burdet II married Elizabeth Rockley and had nine children. Aymer was the eldest and therefore the heir to his fathers estates. A detail has survived which concerns a riot at Birthwaite in 1535 in which Aymer took an active part. This was a turbulent time in history, Henry VIII was on the throne of England, his feud with papal authority over his marriage to Anne Boleyn and his subsequent defiance by placing himself at the head of the English church had alienated many of his subjects. His power enabled him to cause the dissolution of all the monasteries, and the divisions over religion that he caused were widespread. He executed Thomas More in 1535 and Catholics were left fearing for their lives if they did not support the King.

Although we have no details to explain the purpose of the riot in Birthwaite it is common sense to assume that it was religiously oriented. Aymer's politics were strong and his allegiance to the King unquestionable, so much so that soon after, he accused his father, Richard, of treason. Of course it could also have been that Aymer was an ambitious young man and that his desire to inherit his fathers estates was overpowering. Whatever Aymer had planned it backfired somewhat, because a Royal pardon from Henry VIII was made out to Richard Burdet, dated 1st October 1536. The pardon reads as follows:

"*Pardon. Henry VIII to Richard Burdet of Denby Esq., alias Richard Burdet of Howlande Esq., for all offences and rebellions, insurrections, misprisons, etc.*".

Another document which has survived concerns a George Throckmorton who was interrogated for knowledge of treasonable conversations. Throckmorton mentioned his brother in law, Richard Burdet. Richard Burdet promised himself and his dependants in the Kings service at need in Lord Darcy's command. The document is dated 1st October 1536, after the Royal pardon was issued.

It would appear that Richard was against the King in at least some of his actions, though he never spoke officially about his views, his son Aymer became aware of them and so caused the family rift.

To vent his displeasure Richard decided to divide his estate and so gave his second son, Thomas, the manor of Hoyland. This left Aymer with Denby and Clayton, which seems to imply that Richard had forgiven Aymer somewhat by granting him half of the estate when he could have given it all to Thomas.

Fittingly, Richard died in 1547, the same year as Henry VIII and left:

17 messuages (homes with outbuildings and land attached), 1200 acres of land, 550 meadow, 4000 pasture, 1200 of wood, a water mill, 2 fulling, mills, and £9 10s rent, leaving Aymer, now aged 50 as Lord of the Manor of Denby

DENBY'S MEDIEVAL POT

In 1937, two young children were playing on a plot of land just above where today's village green stands. Whilst digging around, John White and Harry Heath came across one of the few archaeological artefacts found in Denby. Two feet below the surface of the ground, covered by a stone slab they came across a pot which lay in a cavity of rock. On further examination a layer of burnt earth was discovered just above it. The pot was in poor condition and had no bottom but was certainly placed here rather than accidentally buried app.500 years before.

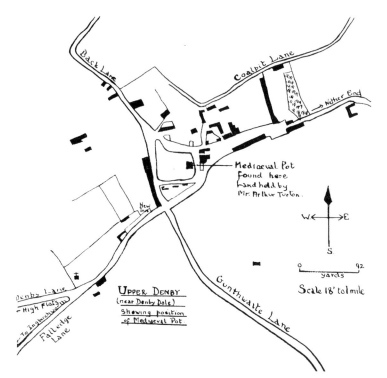

Above. The Mediaval Pot, dated to approximately 1350 - 1400.

Left. Plan showing site on which the pot was discovered.
Courtesy of Tolson Museum, Huddersfield.

It was presented to the Tolson Museum, Huddersfield by Mr L. Taylor of Upper Denby in September 1937 where it remains today, albeit not on display anymore. It is made of local clay and has a rough finish to it. It was certainly not an artefact once likely to be found on a Lords table, and is in extremely poor condition, the broken pieces having been glued back together. It is possible that it was used as a kind of sump, under a fire which heated a cauldron, this might explain the burnt earth, and the absence of a lid which would have been unnecessary as the pot was already covered by the stone slab.

Perhaps the most important piece of evidence that the pot gives us, is that of occupation on the site in the late 14th or early 15th centuries. What form any buildings on the site might have taken is impossible to say, they may have been farm buildings, or perhaps they could have been the lodgings of a labourer and formed part of the original site of the village of Denby.

One can only wander at what else may lay hidden under today's buildings, roads and fields which if discovered might point the way to a clearer understanding of the as yet hidden past of Denby.

BURDET OF BIRTHWAITE & DENBY

Thomas Burdet the son of Richard Burdet II and brother of Aymer had been granted the manor of Hoyland as a result of Aymer's accusation concerning their fathers treason. Thomas preferred to live at Birthwaite and can be found here in 1541. He was probably responsible for the foundation of the Hall which was certainly in use by 1585 after his son and heir, Francis had taken over.

A bond dated 12th August 1546 informs us that at the time of Richard Burdet II's death, Aymer (Americus) was living in Birthwaite and that Thomas resided at Denby Hall. Aymer was contracted to pay Thomas £1000 for the Denby manor by an award made by Thomas Wentworth of West Bretton, Arthur Kay of Woodsom and Thomas Sayvell of Etheslay. He was required to agree to the proposal in writing before the next feast of St. Bartholomew. The fact that Hunter gives the date of death for Richard Burdet II as 1547 is probably explained by the date on the catalogue of assets ascertaining to his manor, which was probably released the following year.

Thomas Burdet married Isabel Wentworth, daughter of the Thomas Wentworth mentioned above, it would appear that he, Kay and Saville were the executors in Richard's will and that Thomas had a slight advantage over his brother regarding his fathers last wishes, though Aymer had married the daughter of Thomas Saville!

Thomas, Burdet and William Hawksworth, a yeoman of Gunthwaite were leased land by the Dean and College of Penistone and Birton in a document dated 17th November 1546. The rent was £53 pa. and the two were also to pay the Vicar of Penistone £4 per quarter and maintain the chapel of St. John the Baptist a little way distant from the town.

BURDET OF BIRTHWAITE

By 1523 the Burdet family had a landed interest in the manor of Birthwaite. The Rockley family held the estate, and it was the marriage of Richard Burdet II to Elizabeth Rockley that brought the area into the Burdet demesne.

The following four heirs to the manors belonging to Thomas Burdet were all named Francis, the first, son of Thomas, being born in 1548. A gradual decline befell the family and when the fourth Francis inherited in 1643 he also inherited debts of £1775 accrued by his father, Francis III who had also given his personal estate and profits of his lands to his Uncle, Robert Rockley.

Francis IV fared little better than his father and is said to have been a 'profligate man'. He had borrowed up to as much as £4000 from his neighbour Sir Thomas Wentworth before 1675 and had a large illegitimate brood of children by a woman named Ann Watkins. He sold off his large estates during the course of his life, Hoyland with lands at Dykeside and Kexborough went to Sir Mathew Wentworth, to help pay for his debts before he died in 1718. In 1665 this Francis was created a baronet, following in the footsteps of his Great Uncle Thomas, brother of the second Francis who we shall return to later.

AYMER BURDET AND THE DENBY ESTATE

Whilst his brother was raising Birthwaite into a greater place, Aymer was doing the same thing at Denby.

Born in 1497 he married Maud, the daughter of Thomas Saville. She bore him at least three children, Henry, son and heir, followed by Richard and Nicholas.

It is interesting to speculate on the attributes of Aymer in his tenure as Lord of the Manor. His politics must have had deep roots, hence his involvement in the riots at Birthwaite and his character must have been passionate and very strong. Whether he carried the vigour and beliefs of his youth into maturity is unknown but it is easy to paint a picture of this man as a strong Lord, highly principled and the terror of the people who farmed his lands.

Aymer died around 1575 aged approximately 78. On his death his son, Henry was required to make the same payment as his father for his estates at Denby to Francis Burdet of Birthwaite. A bond dated 14 April 1575 confirms the payment of £1000. Henry married Elizabeth the daughter of Henry Jackson of London and it was their son that was to finally unite the two most prominent families in the Denby district.

BURDET OF BIRTHWAITE

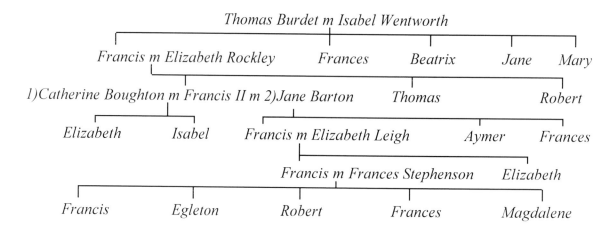

BURDET OF DENBY

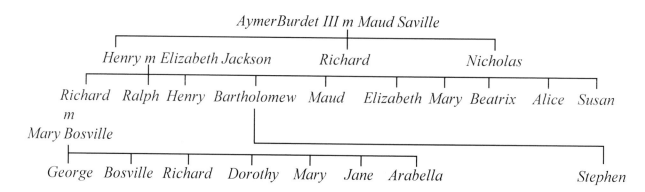

THE SPANISH ARMADA

Henry Burdet, we know, was alive in 1584, just three years prior to the expected Spanish invasion of England in 1587. Believing that the invasion would come in the December, a Council of War was held in November where it was decided that all private gentlemen with a certain yearly income must take up arms and armour and do their duty, or, find another man to take their place. Also each township, would, according to its rateable value, pay and equip a number of soldiers. An army of 130,000 men answered the call for what turned out to be a false alarm. Santa Cruz died on the point of sail from Spain and the invasion was delayed for 6 months. As most of us know, Francis Drake, Frobisher, Effingham and Hawkins destroyed the Spanish Armada in 1588 and the invasion scare was over. Denby supplied six men for the cause:

Private Men :	Thomas Jenkynson	(pikeman) & his man Richard Willmson
	John Michell	(pikeman)
Town Soldiers:	Raufe Clayton	(archer)
	Richard Owdom	(caliver)
	Laurence Hawksworth	(caliver)

(NB: a caliver was a kind of light musket).

The muster took place in Barnsley on 4th December 1587 under the command of Richard Wortley and George Woodruff. The muster comprised 71 gentlemen and 70 town soldiers.

THE LINEAGE OF MARY BOSVILLE

Up until approximately 1460 the Bosville estates at Gunthwaite had been leased and re-leased to various tenants but around this time the manor settled upon a younger branch of the family. It was John Bosville of Newhall and Ardsley who became Lord of Gunthwaite, the family follows thus:

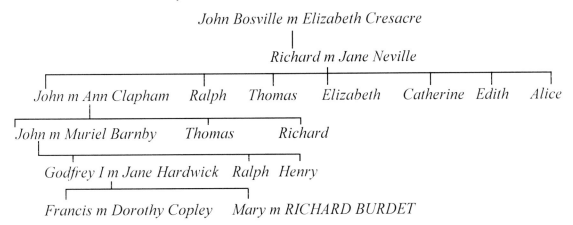

Godfrey I, the great, great grandson of John, was the first member of the family to patronise the Gunthwaite estates, although in his will he styles himself of Beighton. He was born in 1519 and died in 1580 and in that time raised the stature of Gunthwaite significantly. In 1550 he was involved in a lawsuit regarding his lands in the parish with William Turton of Denby, Ottiwel Mashden and John Burdet. He bought the manor of Oxspring and was granted by his brother the rectory, manor and advowson of Penistone church. He was also responsible for the construction of the present barn at Gunthwaite Hall. The barn, today considered by most to be the finest example of its type in the district was built around the middle of the 16th century and it is reputed that a boy served his apprenticeship by making all the wooden pegs which held the beams together.

The barn is immense, having 7100 square feet of floor space and its distinctive black and white timber and plaster work above the 9 ft. walls still evoke memories of four hundred years ago. It was claimed that a wagon and six oxen could turn round inside it.

Godfrey's wife preceded him to the grave and his only son, Francis succeeded on his death. Francis died when he was approximately 30 years old (by 1596) without an heir and it was on the son of his Uncle Ralph that the estates were settled. Francis's sister, Mary, became, along with her other sisters his coheir and her marriage to Richard Burdet of Denby, sometime around 1580 not only unified the two powerful families but increased their influence on the lands around them. It was the four husbands of the sisters of Francis Bosville who inherited the right of presentation of the vicar at Penistone church. Richard Burdet, who was still alive in 1612 had at least 7 children, George the son and heir being born in 1580:

Gunthwaite Barn, circa 1950.

Gunthwaite Barn, present day.

Example of a Denby and Gunthwaite boundary marker, still in Denby in its original position.

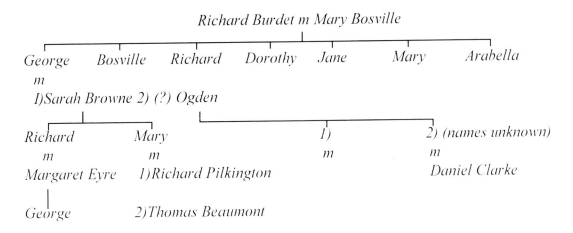

Richard Burdet m Mary Bosville

George   Bosville   Richard   Dorothy   Jane   Mary   Arabella
m
1)Sarah Browne 2) (?) Ogden

Richard   Mary   1)   2) (names unknown)
   m   m   m   m
Margaret Eyre 1)Richard Pilkington   Daniel Clarke

George   2)Thomas Beaumont

The first Godfrey Bosville not only spent more time than his predecessors at Gunthwaite but also more time in the law courts, disputing land boundaries and rights of way, for example :

A bill was exhibited in the court of the Lord President of the North by: William Turton (again), John Claiton and Edward Woodcock of Denby, complaining that Godfrey had used his power to stop a footpath from Denby to Penistone, where their parish church was and also another one which led to Thurlstone. The petitioners alleged that they were only poor men and that he was, 'a man of great mastership and friendship', and asked for redress.

A document of 1566 details some of the lands and boundaries in dispute: A boundary from Crawhill in Gunthwaite was the dividing line for lands at Denby, held by Richard Marshall at a place called 'Butcroft'. Others mentioned are 'Longgrene' to 'Southcroft' at Denby, held by John Jenkynson and lands which abutted Denby held by farmers in the employ of Godfrey Bosville such as Thomas Bower and the Hawksworth family. It seems Godfrey was possessive of his lands, perhaps as a result of the years of neglect by his ancestors which may have led to local inhabitants utilising his land for their ends.

In the time of King James I (1603-1625) the Burdet claim to their manorial rights at Clayton was disputed. Barten Allott, Richard Clayton, Nicholas Hawksworth and Ralph Clayton opposed George Burdet and were able to air their grievances. In 1618, another suit was made against George, this time by the inhabitants of Denby, comprising:

George Hurst   (Dighton, yeoman)
John West   (Denby, yeoman)
John Blagburn   (Denby, son and heir of Robert dec. and John Micklethwaite)
Thomas Clayton   (Clayton, tanner)
Thomas Haugh   (Over Bagden, Denby)
John Shaw   (Bargh, clothier)

The suit concerns property rights claimed at Denby, which were purportedly given to the claimants by William de Denby, lands which George Burdet believed were his. The claimants suggested that George was 'pretending' to be as powerful a Lord as his ancestors, but that he had no right to claim these lands for himself. The suit finishes with the claimants agreeing to support each other and their heirs in resisting the claims made by Burdet.

CIVIL WAR

The death in 1625 of James I (two years before the construction of the chapel of ease in Denby, considered later) brought his son, Charles I to the throne. One of the most turbulent periods in English history was less than twenty years away. When at length Parliament declared war on the King the country was thrown into chaos. Godfrey Bosville II, grandson of Ralph Bosville had abandoned Gunthwaite as a residence and lived at Wroxall in Warwick where he was a member of parliament, he married Margaret Greville, which meant that one of his brothers in law was Arthur Haselrig. In January 1642, the King attempted to arrest five MP's at the House of parliament, John Pym, John Hampden, Denzil Holles, William Strode and Arthur Haselrig - Godfrey's brother in law. For those of you wondering, Oliver Cromwell was not involved in this action as depicted in the film starring Richard Harris, do not believe everything Hollywood' has to say! These MP's escaped or to use the King's own words,

"all the birds have flown",

only to return once the King had abandoned London as a stronghold, to a rapturous reception. The Kings standard was raised in Nottingham in 1642 and Godfrey was named as one of the Deputy Lieutenants for Warwickshire on the side of parliament.

Being a large landholder he was, reputedly, able to raise an army of 1000 strong and the story goes that not one of these men was under 6 feet in height, propaganda perhaps? though they could have been known as the Yorkshire regiment 'the Havercake lads'. Godfrey took to praying and became chaplain to his men. At this time a regiment of 'Roundhead' soldiers were stationed at Gunthwaite, probably housed in the long barn, whilst there, many were infected with typhoid fever and died. It is believed that they were buried in a mass grave by the giant oak, near the hall.

The King was eventually defeated and brought to trial in 1648 when Godfrey Bosville was named as one of the High Court of justice for the trial. However he never attended, implying that he was not in favour of executing Charles. He died in 1658, leaving his son William as his heir. Oliver Cromwell's death in 1658 signalled the end of the Protectorate and paved the way for the restoration of the monarchy. In 1660 William Bosville made his required declaration and was pardoned by King Charles II for the part he played in the parliamentary army. He and his wife retired to Gunthwaite where both died within the next two years.

Shortly after this, two acts of parliament were passed putting the militia on a different level. Every person who had an income of £500 pa, derived from property of held personal estate to the value of £6000 was required to provide, equip and support one horseman. Others of lesser wealth, property income £50 or personal estate £600 provided a pikeman or musketeer. The services of the standing army were dispensed with, leaving the militia as the country's military strength.

A regiment commanded by Sir Michael Wentworth in 1680 consisted of the following men from Denby:

Robert Blackburn	(musketeer) NB.	Thomas Burdet	(musketeer)
Samuel Clayton	(musketeer)	John Hawksworth	(musketeer)
Thomas Hague jnr.	(musketeer)		

(NB : The old barn at Papist Hall farm still has small musket holes or bullet holes in the walls dating from the time of the Civil War. The Robert mentioned above could well be the son of the Robart who built the barn.)

For disobedience or breach of discipline, Magistrates had the power to inflict penalties on the offenders. Others in the regiment were drawn from other local villages such as, Skelmanthorpe, Clayton West, Cumberworth and High Hoyland.

THE BURDET DECLINE

What of the Burdet's during this time? Of their allegiance during the war I have been unable to trace anything to date, though with their close alliances with the Bosville's it would be hard to see them as anything other than parliamentarians.

George Burdet and his first wife had a son and a daughter, Richard and Mary. His second marriage produced at least two more children, one of whom married Daniel Clarke, the curate of Denby. His eldest son, Richard was born in 1610 and was still alive in 1684, though he was not mentioned in the Hearth Tax of 1672, but the fortunes of the family had not been as favoured as those of the Bosville's and by 1643 William Saville of Thornhill was Lord of the Manor.

Richard Burdet IV had sold out for £1500, his estates in Denby along with some lands in Finningley. The Burdet hold on Denby as Lords of the Manor was now over, but the family did continue to live at the Hall and were still very affluent members of the village as we will see from the Hearth Tax, discussed in the next chapter.

THE 17th & 18th CENTURIES & BURDET TO PRESENT

The sale of the Burdet Manor of Denby, did not mean a wholesale evacuation of the village by the family. The extent of their lands is perhaps illustrated by the following quote: 'It was said that the Burdet family could ride from Denby to Barnsley without leaving their own land.'

From 1643 the lands were held by the Saville's of Thornhill and their trustees, and later, according to the 19th century trade directories, the Lord of Scarborough was Lord of the Manor. Although some of the philanthropic Saville family appear in old documents, for instance, the Enclosure Award, their dealings with Denby were limited, they were not Lords of the Manor in the Burdet sense of the word as more and more of the ordinary people had become landholders themselves, by the 17th and 18th centuries.

The Lord of Scarborough could well have been a Saville, though up to press I have been unable to confirm this.

Hearth Tax

Hearth Tax or 'Chimney Money' as it was also known began in 1662, charging people 2 shillings per hearth, paid twice yearly, except for those exempted on the grounds of poverty.

HEARTH TAX - DENBY 1672

1	Mr Barnby	5		31	John Dawson	1
2	Thomas Clayton	6		32	Richard Marshall Snr.	2
3	Widow Burdett	1		33	John Wood	1
4	Tobias Burdett	4		34	John Thomson	5
5	John Clayton	3		35	Joseph Bayley	2
6	Mr Cotton	7		36	Edward Goodall	2
7	John Lyndley	1		37	Joseph Shaw	1
8	Thomas Burdett	5		38	Ralph Swift	2
9	Richard Hawkesworth	5		39	Abraham Mosley	3
10	John (?)	3		40	Richard Micklethwaite	2
11	Thomas Burdett	1		41	Francis West	1
12	George Burdett	2		42	Ralph Horn	2
13	Thomas Hage	5		43	Richard Hanwell	2
14	Joseph Hinchcliff	1		44	Thomas Haigh	4
15	Thomas Shillitoe	1		45	Timothy Booth	1
16	Widow Moorhouse	1		46	Lawrence (Hide?)	1
17	William Moore	1		47	(Jennit?) Hatfield	1
18	Walter Poe	1		48	William Gaunt	1
19	John (Menster?)	1		49	Joseph Pollard	1
20	Emor Burdett	3		50	Samuel Gawber	1
21	Thomas Jessop	1		51	Rodger (Rodes?)	1
22	Thomas Crowther	1		52	Thomas Gaunt	2
23	Godfrey Charlesworth	1				
24	John Gawber	1		Total	115	
25	Widow Robinson	3				
26	Elihu Ward	3				
27	Joseph Mosley	3				
28	Thomas Marshall Jnr.	3				
29	Richard Priest	1				
30	John Shaw	1				

From it we are able to determine the size of a persons house by the number of hearths it contained. The more hearths in a house the wealthier the occupant and so subsequently a social order can be obtained. It must also be remembered that the place known as Denby at this time encompassed what is now Denby Dale and other small hamlets now having a separate identity.

There are at least two surviving copies of the tax roll, one in the Public Record Office in London and the other somewhere in Wakefield. They differ slightly, the list printed on the latter page is my transcription from the copy in London. The Wakefield copy contains the name of William Hamshire who had 1 hearth, but who was exempt from charges on the grounds that his hearth was damaged.

Mr Cotton had 9 hearths and would have been a very prominent citizen of the village. In the Wakefield copy he is recorded as having 9 hearths, though two were not yet finished. In the London copy he is recorded as having only 7. A note at the end of the Wakefield copy instructs the final written copy to be adjusted. William Cotton was a great ironmaster, who lived in various places in the district, including an estate at Darton called the Hague. He had evidently moved to Denby late in life, for a note in 'Hunters - Life of Oliver Heywood' tells us that he died only three years later and was buried at Penistone on the 17th March 1675.

Six Burdet families are listed, including Thomas Burdet who is recorded as living at Denby Hall in other sources. It is also interesting to note that the names of Joseph Hinchcliffe and Thomas Shillitoe appear, two years before their families became embroiled in accusations of witchcraft.

Other family names begin to appear which were to continue to have connections with Denby to the present day. It should also be noted that Rock House, built 1684 and Manor Farm cottage, built 1677 were not a part of the village at this time. The document was signed by Robert Moorhouse and Mathew Burdet who were either witnesses or inspectors.

A number of Burdet's can be found in the Penistone Parish registers around the middle of the 17th century. Unfortunately the records do not go back far enough to enable an easy connection with the last Lord of the Manor, Richard, or his son George but I believe that at least some of the following were the sons of George:

Baptisms

Name	Father	Year born
Gamielli	Delariver	1648
Sara	Emoria	1651
Thomas	?	1653
Tobias	?	1656
Mathew	?	1659
Joseph	?	1659

Marriages

1653	Norman Burdet/Maria Rich
1659	Tobias Burdet/Maria Dowegill

Burials

1652	Nicola Burdet
1659	Mathew Burdet of Delariver
1662	Mathius Burdet
1677	Tobias Burdet

From this it would appear that Delariver and Emoria (possibly another way of spelling Aymer) are the most likely candidates for a direct descent. Emoria or Emor as he is called in the Hearth Tax roll had three hearths but that he was alive and married in 1651 would indicate that by 1672 he was an old man. Delariver does not appear in the tax, though this could simply be because of his death in the years prior to it. Records from Cathill Hall, Hoylandswaine, record that a Jane Sotwell, daughter of Richard Sotwell married Delariviere Burdet of Denby in about 1630. There is also mention of a Jane who married a George Burdet of Carhead around 1600.

We know that the family continued to live at the Hall for some generations after the sale of their estates, it is therefore likely that one of these two was the father of the Thomas living at the Hall in the late 17th century and also of his possible brothers, Jacobi, Tobias, Riccoudi, Marcus and Mathew.

The problem of connecting this enormous family together is compounded when one considers the amount of Burdet's ignored by official pedigrees in library's and so I will try and stick with the ones recorded in the Hearth Tax.

Thomas Burdet as we have already seen had a house with 5 hearths, Tobias had 4. These two had bigger houses (or farmsteads) than any other members of their family. Though not conclusive, I believe the pedigree must continue something like this:

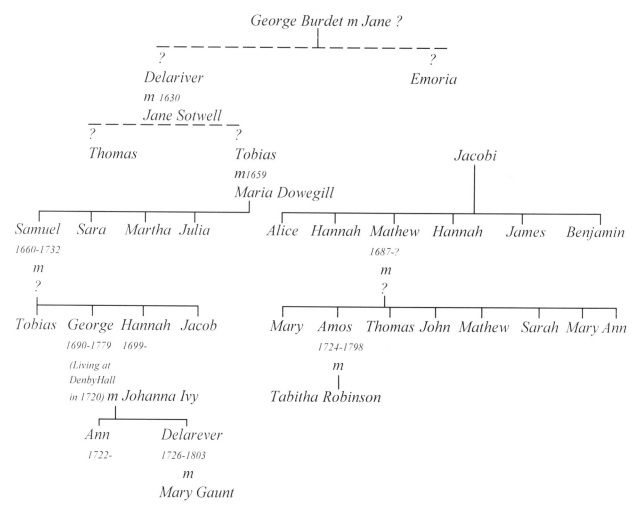

A Thomas Burdet appears in the Penistone marriage register in 1682, where it is recorded that Elizabeth Blackburn was to become his wife. The Blackburn family resided at Papist Hall in Lower Denby. According to 'Hunter' the family were Catholics, one of them acting as agent for the Duke of Norfolk in the management of his estates.

The long barn, (below), was built in 1633 by Robart Blackburn, though it was rebuilt in 1845 as can be seen from the date stone on the wall, by William Smith. Three small windows in the long barn, inner court side, are reputed to be musket holes dating from the time of the Civil War, the barn itself is stone flagged and has a wooden rafter roof. The survival of the musket holes would seem to suggest that the barn was only renovated by William Smith and not wholly rebuilt.

The long barn at Papist Hall built in 1633 and renovated in 1845.

The monument to Robart Blackburn and William Smith, built into the inner court wall.

The current abode of Mr George Wilby was built in 1832, presumably by William Smith. It is reputed that an underground passage leading from an old cellar comes out in Gunthwaite, a staunch Roundhead stronghold. To Mr Wilby's knowledge no such tunnel exists, but the story probably emanates from the time of the Civil War when refuge and flight were necessary contingents.

In 1706 a land lease was made between Thomas Burdet, Phillip Burdet and Robert Blackburn of Denby, presumably this was the Thomas who had married Elizabeth Blackburn, his brother Phillip and either his father or brother in law Robert. Robert Blackburn died in 1716 leaving all his lands at Denby to his brother, Benjamin.

According to Hunter, in the mid 19th century the 'Miss Walkers of Leeds' held the Hall, and were representatives of the Blackburn family.

Hunter also recorded that, "Over the gate is carved a passage from the book of proverbs: Wisdom cryeth at the gates at the entry of the city, at the coming in of the door'."

Sir Francis Burdet of Ramsbury

Born in 1770, he was living in Paris at the time of the French Revolution returning to Britain in 1793. In 1802 he was elected as an MP for Middlesex, after a series of political battles where he won and lost office he was elected MP for Westminster. He was noted for being outspoken and radical in his policies, he was imprisoned in 1810 for breach of Parliamentary privilege and again for his comments about repression at Peterloo in 1819. He became a supporter of Peel in his latter days until his death in 1844. His daughter, Angela Burdet Coutts became the richest heiress in Europe being also the granddaughter of Thomas Coutts, the banker. What has the latter to do with Denby?

According to oral evidence handed down, this remarkable and noteworthy man occasionally visited Denby and its district to see his relatives. How then could Sir Francis be related to the Denby Burdet's?

My investigations are as yet incomplete but at the moment it would seem that the connection could involve the Birthwaite branch of the family, let us just refresh ourselves with the necessary details of that family:

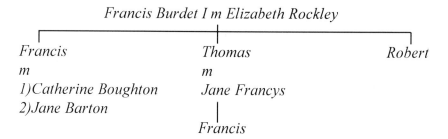

Francis Burdet I m Elizabeth Rockley

Francis	*Thomas*	*Robert*
m	*m*	
1)Catherine Boughton	*Jane Francys*	
2)Jane Barton		
	Francis	

In 1619 Thomas Burdet was created a baronet by James I, with the title of Thomas Burdet of Bramcote. If, as I currently believe, it was the Thomas son of Francis Burdet I of Birthwaite then it would seem that he married Jane Francys who brought to the marriage the estates at Foremark in Derbyshire which became their home. Thomas's son, Francis built and endowed the church of Foremark where both he and his wife were buried. He was succeeded by his son Robert who outlived his own issue, where upon his death in 1716, his grandson, Robert inherited. This Sir Robert Burdet held the title for 80 years and also outlived both his sons, and it was the Sir Francis mentioned above who took over the Baronetcy and lands.

Sir Francis inherited his Ramsbury estates in 1800 following the death of his mothers sister, Lady Jones. Under the terms of the will he was compelled to take the name 'Jones' and for a few months was known as Sir Francis Burdet Jones but he quickly reverted back.

The line continued thus:

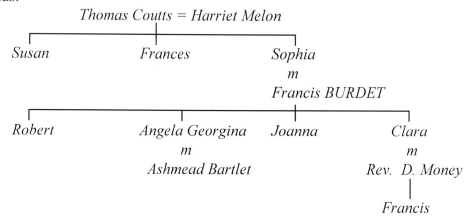

Thomas Coutts = Harriet Melon

Susan	*Frances*	*Sophia*
		m
		Francis BURDET

Robert	*Angela Georgina*	*Joanna*	*Clara*
	m		*m*
	Ashmead Bartlet		*Rev. D. Money*
			Francis

In 1801 Sir Francis was a wealthy landed proprietor owning both Ramsbury and Foremark, receiving £40,000 pa. from lands alone, quite apart from his wifes fortune.

Sophia Burdet Coutts died after a long invalidity in June 1844, Sir Francis died in January 1844, they were buried in the Burdet vault in Ramsbury church. His son Robert succeeded but died unmarried in 1880 and the son of Sir Francis's brother, Jones Burdet inherited.

Harriet Melon married Thomas Coutts in 1815, he died in 1822 and afterwards she remarried to the Duke of St. Albans. Thomas Coutts left his great wealth to Harriet who between 1822 and 1831 gave each of their daughters £10,000 pa. Harriet died aged 60 when her husband, the Duke, was only 36. She had taken a liking to Angela Burdet Coutts and left her whole fortune to her and her son if she had one. Unfortunately Angela and her sister Joanna died childless and it was Francis, the son of Clara who inherited the family titles.

Angela Burdet Coutts was born in 1814 and married late in life to an American, Ashmead Bartlet, under the terms of her grandmothers will she could not now inherit the Coutts fortune leaving Clara's son Francis as sole heir. By a family arrangement two fifths of the Coutts income was left to the Baroness for her lifetime.

Diana Orton wrote the biography of Angela named 'Made of Gold' before the Baroness died on the 30th December 1906. She was buried under the floor of the nave inside the west door of Westminster Abbey.

Although the Burdet Lords of Denby and Birthwaite became extinct, this branch of the family not only flourished but prospered, if the oral evidence is reliable then Sir Francis and maybe others visited Denby from time to time and did not ignore their more humble relations.

Denby Hall

Denby Hall stands a little way from the road heading towards Cawthorne at Nether Denby. Most of the remaining buildings are comparatively modern with the particular exception of one. The long barn, built in 1698, was originally the living quarters of the Burdet's and their successors. Today the original roof has gone, being replaced by a corrugated iron one and all that remains of this once Lordly Manor House is the shell, now cluttered with farming paraphernalia.

Denby Hall, from a postcard dated 1907.

There is though some conjecture as to the original site of this ancient abode of the Lords of Denby. It could be that a structure was sited on the land where the present Hall stands today for centuries before a stone one replaced it. But another contender for the earliest site of the Hall are the buildings known as Stocks Hall at Lower Denby. Stocks Hall was in existence in 1610 as was Denby Hall, although the map is not specific, the locations in regard to the area and Gunthwaite Hall are broadly correct with today's ordnance survey maps.

A stone or plasterwork coat of arms was reputedly filled in and covered over in one of the bedrooms of Stocks Hall, as to whether it was the Burdet coat of arms, we shall probably never know and without this important piece of evidence the conjecture must go on.

Whatever the history of Stocks Hall, it was certainly an important building at least as far back as 1610, its origins most likely being much older than that. It is possible that it was one of the more affluent residences in the village at the time the Hearth Tax was recorded in 1672. We could then perhaps surmise that if it wasn't the Hall, could it have been the residence of one of the younger Burdet's, perhaps Tobias?

Wherever he lived Tobias was still a wealthy man for his time, his possible brother, Thomas held the Hall and the memories of being Lords of the Manor were not long past. It could be reasoned that Richard Burdet's sale of his lands in 1643 was brought about during the Civil War by the families Royalist connections, but again this is only conjecture. At a time when father fought son and neighbour fought neighbour it is not an unreasonable possibility.

Tobias's grandson, George was living at Denby Hall at the time of his marriage to Johanna Ivy, thereby confirming Tobias's connections with his ancestors who held Denby from at least the 13th century. By now the Hall was just a working farm and not a base for the Lord to hold his council and manage his estates, as it has remained to this day.

George's son was Delarever Burdet, a name which although conspicuous by its rarity from early pedigrees became synonymous with these later Burdet's.

Written in many different forms, presumably at the discretion of the author ie:

Delarever, Delariver, Delariviere, Dallyriver and Dallyriviere,

Its literal meaning when translated into French is 'of the river'. It would be reasonable to speculate that the name arrived with the family from France during the Norman conquest, yet as mentioned, it does not appear in the early pedigrees. Why then did the family adopt such a name from the late 16th and early 17th centuries? The reason is now lost, although I am informed there was a reason, but unfortunately the gentleman who knew it died many years before I began researching the history of the village.

It was in the time of Delarever's father, George, that a petition was made for the inhabitants of Denby, Silkstone, Hoylandswaine and the neighbourhood regarding the condition of the wooden bridge at what is now Denby Dale, then Denby. The bridge which crossed the Dearne by the Corn Mill, (demolished in the 1970's) was used daily by pack horses, but floods destroyed it in 1706 and trade was thus being hampered as other routes had to be taken. It was decided that a new structure should be built, this time in stone and the sum of £7 10s was paid to Godfrey Bosville to begin the work, though a further £40 was needed, raised by the local people to complete the task.

The Burdet family continued to steadily decline throughout the 18th century. Their tenure at the Hall ended and most of them became farmers or tradesmen, many of which can be found in the listings reproduced in the chapter on the nineteenth century later in this book.

George Burdet seems to have been the last Burdet to live in the Hall. He died in 1779 and is listed in the register as living at Denby Hall. Delarever's lineage continued thus:

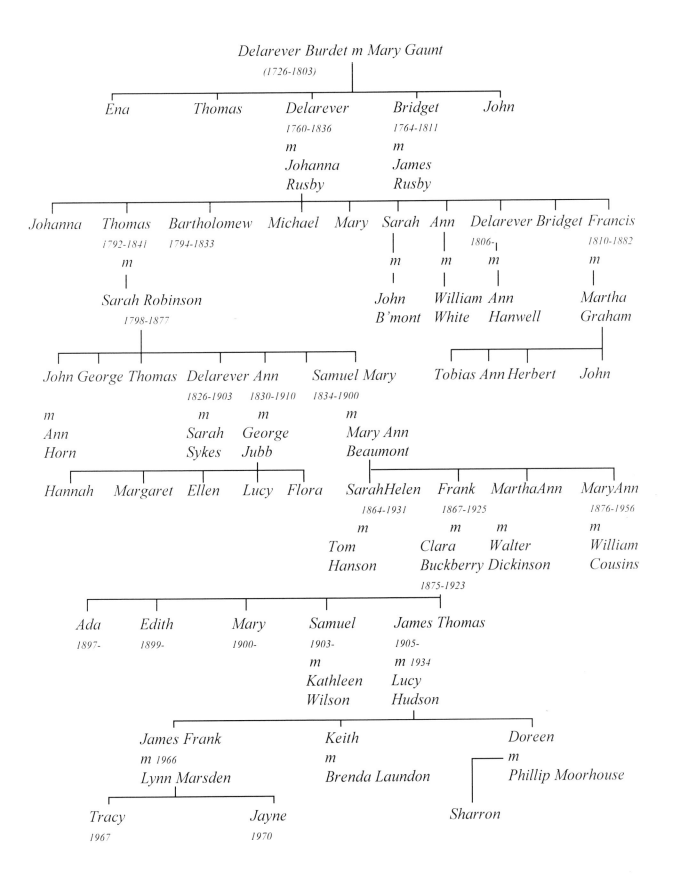

Delarever Burdet m Mary Gaunt
(1726-1803)

Ena   Thomas   Delarever   Bridget   John
                 1760-1836   1764-1811
                 m   m
                 Johanna   James
                 Rusby   Rusby

Johanna Thomas   Bartholomew Michael Mary Sarah Ann Delarever Bridget Francis
         1792-1841 1794-1833   1806-   1810-1882
         m   m   m   m   m
         Sarah Robinson   John   William Ann   Martha
         1798-1877   B'mont White   Hanwell   Graham

John George Thomas Delarever Ann   Samuel Mary   Tobias Ann Herbert John
                    1826-1903 1830-1910 1834-1900
m   m   m   m
Ann   Sarah   George   Mary Ann
Horn   Sykes   Jubb   Beaumont

Hannah Margaret Ellen Lucy Flora   SarahHelen   Frank   MarthaAnn MaryAnn
                                        1864-1931   1867-1925   1876-1956
                                        m   m   m   m
                                        Tom   Clara   Walter   William
                                        Hanson   Buckberry Dickinson Cousins
                                                     1875-1923

Ada   Edith   Mary   Samuel   James Thomas
1897-   1899-   1900-   1903-   1905-
                              m   m 1934
                              Kathleen   Lucy
                              Wilson   Hudson

         James Frank   Keith   Doreen
         m 1966   m   m
         Lynn Marsden   Brenda Laundon   Phillip Moorhouse

Tracy   Jayne   Sharron
1967   1970

41

The present dwelling at Denby Hall which was rebuilt in 1923.

Manor Farm Cottage, built by Joseph Mosley in 1677.

Rock House on Bank Lane, built in 1684.

A Quaker element was brought into the family by the marriage of Samuel to Mary Ann Beaumont and subsequently the family were more numerous in High Flatts.

The Thomas Burdet, son of the second Delarever was not only a joiner and wheelwright in Upper Denby (possibly a forerunner to John Milnes) but also the landlord of the Star public house.

The family retained woodworking oriented occupations up until the early 20th century, alongside farming and shopkeeping and other village trades.

Whilst these ex-Lords of the Manor were readjusting to more ordinary lives the village of Denby was expanding rapidly. Some of the earliest buildings in the village dating from the latter half of the 17th century. Farms such as Denroyd and Gunthwaite Gate were constructed, possibly on older previously used sites and cottages were built to house an expanding population.

Pinfold house was built in 1795 on the site where there were once two pinfold's. The term 'pinfold' is of ancient origin, in old English, 'punfald', which gave its name to the 'pinder', the man responsible for rounding up stray cattle and impounding them until their rightful owners arrived, when after paying a toll they were allowed to take them away.

For the Burdet's the old days were just distant memories, the family had spread around the district, cousins lived in Penistone, Barnsley, Huddersfield and nearly all the villages in between, many of them would have been ignorant to the exact details of the families illustrious past, but perhaps visits made by Sir Francis Burdet of Ramsbury and Foremark reminded them that the name Burdet was something to be proud of. Today the name has dwindled in its regularity in Denby and around the area but some of these direct ancestors of the Lords of the Manors of Denby and High Hoyland do still live in Denby and Denby Dale and would be very pleased if you called them Sire or M'Lady.

WITCHCRAFT

Between the years 1533 and 1712 more than 4000 men, women and children stood on trial, accused of witchcraft, or of being in league with the Devil. King James I even wrote his own guide book on how to deal with this menace, entitled 'Demonology'. An act was passed in the early part of the 17th century against 'conjuration, witchcraft and dealing with evil and wicked spirits' and as a result 'witch hunting' became a popular and frequently beneficial sport. Evidence to bring a person to trial was not easy to obtain and so the Courts relaxed the rules to a large degree in order to obtain results. In England, torture was not technically a part of the judicial system, but an unpleasant time was bound to ensue. Across Europe witches were burned, in England they were usually hung, but these were the end results after barbaric forms of torture had obtained confessions from those on trial, many given whether it was the truth or not just to gain the relief from torture brought about by death. Generally females were accused, being considered at the time to be more susceptible to the charms of the Devil, they would then be stripped and searched for the 'Devils Mark'. Mathew Hopkins, the 'witchfinder general' between 1644 and 1646 used sleep and food deprivation and binding his victims in painful positions for hours as a means to extract a confession. There was of course also the 'ducking stool' or 'cucking stool' where a witch would be proved by her ability to float on the water, if she sank and died, then she was guiltless ! Cuckstool Road in Denby Dale, survives to this day to remind us of this activity, down in Heywood Bottom, where the river still flows.

Against this somewhat hysterical background two women from Denby found themselves accused and were taken to a Barnsley gaol to wait for their hearing at Wooley before Darcy Wentworth Esq. to answer for their alleged indiscretions. The two were Ann Shillitoe (wife of Thomas) and Susan Hinchcliffe (wife of Joseph). Their accuser was Mary Moor, a spinster aged 16.

Fred Lawton in his 'Historical Notes of Skelmanthorpe and District' gives the following transcription of the evidence brought before the Court: Mary Moor gave the following evidence;

"That Susan said to Ann,

'If thou cans't but get young Thomas Haigh to buy three pennyworth of indico, and look him in the face when he gives it thee, and touch his locks, we shall have power enough to take life.'

Susan also said,

'Nanny, wilt thou not go today and make hay at Thomas Haigh's?'

Ann answered,

' If thou cans't but bring nine bits of bread away and nine bits of butter in thy mouth, we shall have power enough to take the life of their goods. They need not be in such pomp, for we will neither leave him cow nor horse at house.'

Ann asked Susan,

'Mother, did you do Dame Haigh any hurt?'

Susan replied,

'That I did, for after I touched the edging of her skirt, she stepped not many steps after. I shortened her walk.'

Mary Moor continues, with details of a previous conversation between the two accused,

Susan said to Ann,

'I think I must give this Thomas Bramhall over, for they tie so much wighen, (the rowan that the witches hated, formerly used by the Druids in ancient times) about him, I cannot come to my purpose, else I could have worn him away once in two years.'

Ann replied,

'Thou are too far worn'

Susan then said to her daughter,

'Nanny, did not thou hear that Timothy Haigh had like to have been drowned I'th Water Hall dyke?'

Mary Moor didn't hear her answer, Susan then said,

'I led him up and down the moor, with an intention that he should either have broke his neck or have drowned himself; but at last his horse threw him, and he then went over the bridge, and I had a foot in. How he got over the bridge I cannot tell, except the Lord led him by the hand. I had him not at that time. But the next time let both the horse and him look both to themselves'.

Ann then asked her mother if she had ever done John Moor any hurt, her mother replied yes and said,

'I took the life of two swine and did hurt to a child.'

Mary Moor also heard Susan say to Ann that if her father had but touched Martha Haigh, before she had spoken to him, they could have had power enough to take away her life, to which Ann replied,

'There is no time bye-past.'

Mary Moor also said that about the middle of July last past, going to borrow a linewheel, she heard Ann say to Susan,

'I saw my father play such a trick last night as I never saw in my life, he asked for butter, and their came butter onto his knee in a wooden saucer.'

Susan replied,

'That was but a little. Hast thou lived in this house so long, and never saw any of thy father's tricks? Dost not know that thy father went to John Walkers to steime (order) a pair of shoes, and he would not let him have them without he had money in his hand; but he never made pair after. Likewise he went to George Copley's to steime a waistcoat cloth, and he would not let him have it without he had silver in his hand; and because he would not let him have it he never made piece after but two. If anybody would not let them have what they wanted they would take the life of anybody.'

Susan said to Ann, that Joseph Hinchcliffe was as ill as they, but would not be seen in it. He bore it far off. Ann also said that if they were known they might be hanged, but Susan replied that no hemp would hang them. Ann said they might be burnt to which Susan answered,

'Nay, they would never tell until they died.'

Mary Moor also heard Ann say,

'I'll warrant ye thou shall say little when thou comes before the bench.'

To make matters even more complicated another statement was taken from Timothy Haigh of Denby which said: he was present when Mary Moor, (the chief witness!) did vomit a piece of bended wire and piece of paper with two crooked pins in it,

A Witch begging raw materials from the Gravedigger.

45

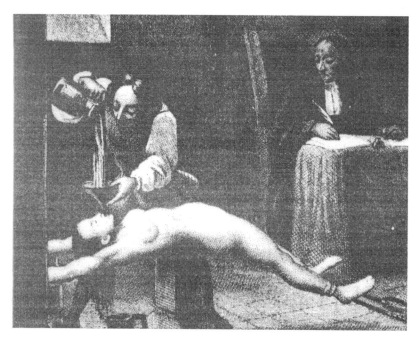

and 'hath at several other times seen her vomit crooked pins.'

One has to wonder what the villagers and indeed their Church curate, Timothy Kent, made of all the latter! A mother and daughter arrested for alleged crimes of witchery because of the evidence of a 16 year old girl. A girl who had also implicated the husband and father Joseph, only to be accused of evil machinations herself.

The drama could have initially been played out in Lower Denby, the Haigh family living for many generations on the site of the Wagon and Horses Public House. It seems highly likely that a neighbourhood feud had developed between the Hinchcliffe's, Haigh's and Moor's, malicious gossip, government propaganda and the relaxed requirements for evidence by the Courts made this a very easy time for people to settle disagreements by eliminating the other parties involved. Of course, Denby could perhaps have played host to two of the 'Devils Brood' but the evidence points more to the former rather than the latter.

The last execution for witchcraft in England took place in Exeter in 1682, though trials continued until 1712. In Denby a little common sense prevailed and a petition was raised, signed by more than 50 people and addressed to the Magistrates of the West Riding:

'Some of us have well known the said Sussanna and Anna by the space of 20 years and upwards, others of us for 15 years and upwards, others of us for 10 years and upwards. And have by the said space observed and known the life and conversation of the said Sussanna to be not only very sober, orderly and unblameable in every respect but also of good example and very helpful and useful in the neighbourhood according to her poor ability. That she was a constant frequenter of public ordinances while she was able, and to the best of our understanding made conscience of her ways in more than common sort. That we never heard, or had the least ground to suspect her, or her said daughter, to be in any sort guilty of so foul a crime, but do fully believe that the said information against them both is a most gross and groundless (if not malicious) prosecution. And this we humbly certify as our very true apprehensions, as in the sight and presence of Him who will judge the secrets of all our hearts. And as touching the said girl who now informs, some of us could say much concerning her of a quite different nature, but that we judge recrimination to be but an indirect way of clearing the innocent.'

The two women were committed for trial in York at the next assizes, although nothing survived in the records to tell of the outcome. The record itself when last seen, was torn in two, which would seem to indicate that the charges were thrown out. Brian Elliot in his book 'The Making of Barnsley' supplies the answer, he discovered a note in 'Hunters' - 'Life of Oliver Heywood' which completed the story.

Apparently Joseph Hinchcliffe, who was bound over with his wife and daughter, committed suicide on the morning of Thursday 4th February 1675, he wasn't discovered until the following Sunday. Meanwhile, his wife, Susan had died praying on her death bed for her accusers.

It is possible that the statement of Mary Moor was ripped in two because two of the three accused parties had died within six months of their appearance at Wooley and that the case had not yet been heard at York. Given the petition of the villagers it would seen that the shame of the accusations had claimed both their lives, and that the case had been dismissed, yet why had Susan Hinchcliffe died praying on her deathbed for her accusers if the case really had been thrown out?

The last witch in the area of which any record was made was also an inhabitant of Upper Denby. Betty Roberts was alive during the early 19th century, she is described by Fred Lawton, in his 'Historical Notes of Skelmanthorpe and District' thus,

'She was very peculiar looking, and wore a tall peaked bonnet or hat, and a long, dark cloak - something after the familiar pictures of Mother Shipton. She lived in a lone hut, which the boys were terrified to pass, although there was a strange attraction to try and peep in, for they were taught they might see the 'posnet' or small cauldron on the fire, in which she brewed the 'stuff' by which she was enabled to fly up the chimney or through the keyhole. When she was teased she made strange cabalistic signs, as if she were calling the stars to avenge her, at the same time uttering some strange gibberish. As she had no relatives, it was supposed that at one time she had belonged to a wandering tribe of gypsies.'

RELIGION & WORSHIP

THE CHURCH

Denby was originally incorporated into the extensive Parish of Penistone, the church there being built around 1200. The villagers of Denby, therefore had to walk or travel in carts to facilitate their desire for worship and for all the usual services provided by the establishment. In the winter months it was difficult, indeed, nigh on impossible to cross the flooded waters of Scout Dyke in order to reach Penistone. In 1626 the waters of the dyke claimed the lives of 13 parishioners on their way to church, a tragedy, which further resolved the villagers to petition Archbishop Tobias Mathew for a licence to erect a chapel. He agreed and on 12th Dec. 1627, at York he formalised the agreement. Although he was unable to comply with their requests for him to consecrate it, he did allow them licence to perform religious ordinances here without prejudice to the Vicars of Penistone, and also granted them the choir offices. It was Godfrey Bosville (who's father Ralph had bought the advowson of Penistone Church from Elizabeth I) who built it. Unfortunately the only surviving record to tell of the size or design of this building is the tiny representation made on the Enclosure map below dated 1802, though the chapel continued in use until 1844. This building was known as a Chapel of Ease or District Chapel under the diocese of Penistone.

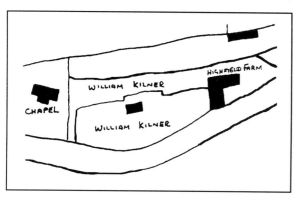

Reproduction of the Enclosure Map of 1802 shows the shape of the chapel thus.

After Ralph Bosville had bought the right of presentation of the Vicar, or advowson, for the rectory of Penistone it passed through his family line by way of his sisters and it was their husbands who were responsible for naming the Vicar.

1602 - Godfrey Copley, 1619 - John Saville Esq., 1633 - George Burdet of Denby, 1635 - George Burdet (again) and in 1642 - Sir William Saville. Hunter, noted that there was probably an irregularity in the double presentation of George Burdet but it is clear from the above how closely involved Penistone Church was with Denby and Gunthwaite and its most prominent families the Burdet's and Bosville's.

The foundation of the Chapel at Denby was therefore guided by very strong hands, probably encouraged by the growing spirit of Puritanism which swept the country during the reigns of James I and Charles I.

Since the Bosville's were puritans it was natural that they should appoint a puritan minister and they chose Charles Broxholme.

The following extract is taken from 'Dransfield's- History of Penistone' and is an extract of the 'De Spiritualibis Pecci of Bagshaw':

" He was a gentleman born, and so one reckons of the lesser (and lower) nobility. His brother was a Parliament man, in and for some place in Lincolnshire. Providence brought him into the ministry ; and in the exercise of it, unto Belper in Derbyshire, Gunthwaite in Yorkshire and Denton in Lancashire, and so to Buxton, noted for its bath, but never so honoured as when he and some of his excellent successors were as preachers and pastors there.

It hath been said that in his time, as there was violent imposition by some on one, so there was violent opposition by some on the other side. This must be said of him, though his principles hindered him being an active conformist, they led him to be a passive and patient non-conformist. As another great man said he might say, his head was too big for a Church door ; till near his end he placed in Chapels : such were those I have named. The violence of those called Cavaliers who too many of them did as one said, hate all manner of purity whatsoever, drove him into Derby, where under Sir John Gell the father, his life was secured."

Broxholme was succeeded by Daniel Clarke in 1635. Clarke was educated at Kings College, Cambridge, where he took his BA degree in 1631 and MA in 1634. Whilst at Denby he married a daughter of George Burdet. Clarke was favourable to the cause of Parliament during the Civil War, he was appointed by them on the 14th March 1643 to leave Denby and officiate in Kirkburton Church and to 'receive the profits of the said vicarage for his paynes, till further orders be taken by both houses of Parliament'. His predecessor at Kirkburton, Gamaliel Whitaker, was displaced by Parliament for following the cause of the King. In a Parliamentary survey, Clarke was described as a 'painful preacher'. He left Kirkburton in approximately 1649.

Up to now no provision had been made for the minister at Denby, but on 6th January 1648 this changed. As the Civil War drew to a close, Colonel Godfrey Bosville (a Parliamentarian) was instrumental in initiating that the heirs of Sir Edward Osborne of Kiveton (deceased), should pay £25 per annum to Denby Chapel and the same sum to Seaton Ross in the East Riding. The money was paid irregularly, but eventually £1000 was paid by the heirs of Osborne to Colonel Bosville.

Daniel Clarke was succeeded by a man named Miller who was subsequently followed by John Crooke, from Sheffield. He settled in Denby whilst acting as its curate. He was a puritan and non-conformist who eventually retired to Wakefield where he died in 1587.

Some time after 1662, the Vicar of Cawthorne, Christopher Wallbank, made an attempt to gain the curacy of Denby by forging a nomination. A certificate recommending him to the people of the village was allegedly signed by, Sir Gervase Cutler, Thomas Barnby, Loy Kett (Vicar of Silkstone), Henry Bubwith, Henry Lewis and others. He was found out and promptly deprived for his efforts.

Timothy Kent took over in 1665 and continued up until his death in 1691. His stone epitaph survives in the Church, written in Latin:

The Monument in the Church commemorating the Rev. Timothy Kent.

The following translation comes from a booklet produced to mark the centenary of the Church in 1945:
"Here Timothy Kent awaits Christ's future coming;
Master of Arts and of this Church a recent minister.
A pastor, honourable and steadfast ; most watchful lest any should wander.
A popular orator, constant, beneficial, and eloquent
His arguments weighty, yet cunning ; how alluring of speech, yet mightier in actions.

A good man, yet greater in writing. Though stone cannot express his peculiar excellences,
The longings of his friends will yet constantly speak.
   Died, 28th August 1691"

The Chapel was augmented in 1738 with £200 given by Rev. Jonathan Perkins (whom we shall return to) to pay for its expenses and provide a salary for the incumbent. In 1739 a further £200 was granted, allocated from the fund known as 'Queen Anne's Bounty'.

The revenues for this had been transferred from a Papal taxation known as 'First Fruits and Tenth's', whereby a person appointed to a living was obliged to pay 10% of his first years income to the Pope. The proceeds were handed over to the Church of England by Queen Anne in 1704 to provide a fund for the relief of the poorer Anglican clergy, by making grants to livings with incomes of less than £10 per annum (raised in 1788 to £35). From 1809 it was paid by Parliamentary grants, after which, in 1816, Denby received a further £1200.

During the eighteenth century some of the Masters of Penistone Grammar school acted as curates at Denby. Historian W. H. Senior noted in the book 'A History of Denby Dale Urban District' that in 1764 Archbishop Drummond found a Jonothan Perkins acting as master of the Grammar school and curate. There appears to be some confusion about an incumbent at Denby with this name. Rev. Moore noted in 1729 a Jonathan Parker, Joseph Hunter named the man Jonothan Parkin and the trade directories of the 19th century note a Jonothan Perkins.

In 1743 Thomas Cockshutt, Vicar of Penistone reported to his Archbishop about matters relating to his parish. It was Jonathan Perkins who supplied the following information:

1) We have 130 families in chapelry of Denby of which 9 are Quakers. No papists or other kind of Dissenters.
2) We have one licensed meeting house for Quakers who assemble every Lords Day to the number of 80. One Elihu Dickinson teaches.
3) We have one Charity School endowed with £5 a year for teaching poor children. Sufficient care is taken to teach them in the principles of Christian religion, according to the doctrine of the Church of England, and to bring them duly to Church.
4) Denby being in the Parish of Penistone, I being Grammar School master there reside in the school-house, having no house or lands belonging to the chapelry of Denby.
5) I do all the duty of the Chapelry myself.
6) I know of none that come to Denby Chapel that are not baptised but I believe that a 100 of competent age come who are not confirmed.
7) Every Sunday and Holy Day and twice on every Lords Day, Divine Service is performed.
8) The first Sunday in every month I catechise in the Chapel and every Saturday in the Grammar School by which means most children and servants in these parts are sufficiently instructed in their catechism.
9) I never administer the Sacrament in the Chapel of Denby, though I believe that there are 200 communicants in our Chapelry most of which receive at different times in the Parish Church.
10) I give open and timely warning of Sacrament being administered at the Parish Church the Sunday before I and the inhabitants take it at Penistone.

The latter was signed by Jonathan Perkins. Adm. 19th July 1731, Deacon, Chester, 26 October 1729. Priest 18 July 1731. Christ's College, Cambridge.

In approximately 1751 Samuel Phipps became curate, prior to becoming Vicar of Penistone, being presented by Godfrey Bosville in 1761. There is also evidence to suggest that by 1780 he was Vicar of

Silkstone.

The Churchwardens presentment for the Denby Chapelry has the following to say, dated 15th June 1750:

"All is well. Our schoolmaster is efficient but we have no ministers house. John Horsfall, Joseph Gaunt, Joseph Rhodes and Wm. Earnshaw, Churchwardens. 1721, July 29th - I Phillip Mitchell, Churchwarden of Penistone, do certify that John Goldthorpe presented at the last visitation for profaning the Sabbath and for not repairing to his Parish Church hath since the visitation duly frequented the said Church as witness my hand Phillip Mitchell."

Francis Haigh became master of the Grammar school in 1751, he was later to aquire the curacy of Denby and those of Bolsterstone and Midhope. Although these curacy's supplemented his income they also caused him to neglect his school duties. In addition to this he became blind during the last 10 years of his life, until he died in 1776. Joseph Horsfall became the next master of the school, though he was negligent in the extreme and was eventually made to resign, whether he preached at Denby is unknown.

Joseph Wood of Nantwich succeeded Horsfall as master until his death in 1836, but his activities at Denby were limited. By at least 1822 John Brownhill had become curate of the Chapel at Denby. He was followed by Brice Bronwin who was the incumbent at the time of Bishop Longley's visitation in 1839.

The Bishop found the Chapel to be in such a, 'filthy and ruinous state' that he ordered it to be pulled down and money raised to rebuild it. In 1844, under Bronwin, a building committee was formed. John Ellis, a builder from High Flatts was paid £1170 to construct a new and bigger Church which was completed in 1845.

This building forms the major portion of the present Church, but consisted of a tower and nave only. The altar was at the east wall of the nave and a gallery surrounded the other three walls; box pews filled the nave, after only a short time the porch was added.

On 12th December 1853 an order in council was signed by Queen Victoria making Denby into a separate Parish, to include the villages of Gunthwaite, Ingbirchworth, High Flatts, Birdsedge and Denby

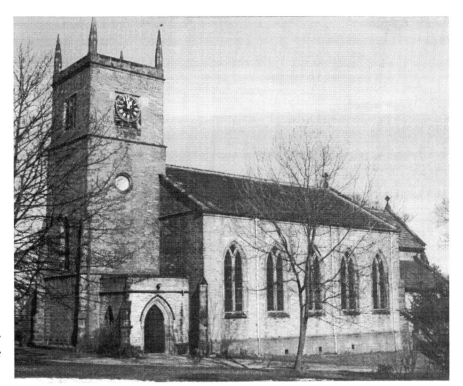

Denby Church, present day. The structure had only a tower and nave in 1845 but has been much altered.

Dykeside (now Denby Dale) all of which were previously under Penistone authority.

Job Johnson of Huddersfield had become curate in 1851, but became Vicar in 1853. He was responsible for the construction of the Vicarage in 1873 at a cost of £1800 (though £2000 is also quoted).

Before the construction of the vicarage the curates had lived in one of the cottages which formed part of the site of 'Highfield Farm'. Though these were probably the late 18th and early 19th century incumbents. The Masters of the Grammar school most likely having lived in Penistone. According to the booklet 'A Stroll Around Denbi' these cottages were originally owned by a J. Micklethwaite, possibly a descendent of the Lords of Ingbirchworth. They were bought in 1781 for £43 by William Kilner, who redeveloped the site. His farm and lands as can be seen from the Enclosure map were the closest to the Chapel.

In later years the adjacent farm, called 'Highfield Farm' and at least one of the cottages became the home of the 'Charlesworth' family. The farm site has been redeveloped in recent times by local building contractor, Joe Price, the name Highfield Farm being dropped in favour of Upper House Fold, which

Denby Scouts with Flat Capped Vicar, Rev. Tibbits.

Scouting was a serious business when this was taken, in 1928 or 1929. The troups were those of Upper Denby Church and members were, from back left: G Booth, C H Roden, F Grange, F Matthews, J Senior, F Booth, vicar the Rev G O Tibbets; M Dearnley, H Kilner, E Turton, J Dronfield, G Hudson, E Dronsfield; D Buckley, D Rusby, D Barber, D Haigh, E Gelder; A Beever, J Fawcett, C Schofield, J Lockwood H Turton, S Schofield, L Shaw, R Taylor. Photo from Dearneside Road, Denby Dale.

Bishop Dedicates Church Clock at Denby

ON Saturday, the parishioners of Denby Parish Church, ncluding members of the local Jrban Council, saw an eighteen-nonth-old ambition fulfilled vhen they took part in the dedi-ation by the Bishop of Pontefract the Rt. Rev. A. H. Morris) of a :lock in the tower.

The clock, which is an eight-lay one, has two dials, each five ... nches across. It has cost ;?v.

Subsc.ptions to date are about :20 short of the total. Two

Picture shows (left to right): Mr. J. Turton (churchwarden), Clr. Kaye, Mr. White, the Bishop of Pontefract, Mr. Colin Crossland (churchwarden), the Vicar and Mr. Waldie.

sisters, Mrs. Annie Haigh and Mrs. Lucy Kaye, have spent the past eighteen months in house-to-house collecting for the clock fund.

A pull on a long cord by the

oldest member of the congrega-tion—eighty-three-year-old Mr. J. R. Waldie—in the ancient porch set in motion the striking mechanism of the clock.

After he had dedicated the clock "in thankful remembrance of the benefactors of the parish," the Bishop, accompanied by the Vicar (the Rev. N. A. Moore), the verger (Mr. R. White), Clr. J. H. Kaye and the churchwardens (representing the subscribers), returned to their places in church to continue a prepared form of service.

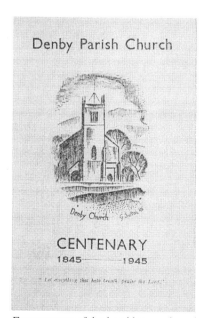

Denby Parish Church

CENTENARY
1845———1945

" Let everything that hath breath praise the Lord."

Front cover of the booklet produced for the Church's Centenary

Local newspaper cutting reporting the instalation of a new clock, probably dating from the mid 1950's

reflects the residential properties created here.

Job Johnson was succeeded by the second Vicar of Denby, Alexander Barrington Orr, of Trinity College, Dublin. In 1887 Reverend Orr formed a Church Council 'in order to promote the harmonious co-operation of Priest and people'. A meeting was held at the Vicarage on Saturday 3rd December 1887 to constitute the same. It was during Rev. Orr's time that a large part of Denby Dykeside was ceded to Cumberworth Parish, this occurred in 1892.

Romeo Edwin Taglis became Vicar in 1894. He was responsible for a large renovation and rebuilding operation about the Church during 1900/1901. The interior of the nave was almost entirely rebuilt. The gallery was taken down, stone pillars and arches were raised, dividing the centre aisle from the North and South portions of the nave. A barrel roof was placed over the centre aisle and a new chancel was built with a crossed rafter roof. The interior of the Church was now a copy of one which the Vicar had seen in Italy. A vestry was added to the South side of the chancel and new pews replaced the old fashioned box pews in the nave. The organ, which had been in the gallery was now put in the chancel against the vestry. Thus rebuilt, the building was re-opened and consecrated on Wednesday, June 19th, 1901.

Rev. Taglis ended his days at Denby, his grave is inscribed:

Romeo Edwin Taglis, Priest, for 32 years Vicar of Denby, died 24 September 1926 aged 67. Also, Margaret his wife, died 11 April 1940 aged 78.

Gervase Tibbits and Reginald Sheard followed Taglis, both becoming integral parts of the community, leading the choir, taking Scout troops and raising money for Church funds.

In Norman Moore's first year of office, 1944, the men of the Parish entirely re-decorated the interior of the chancel and nave. The following year saw the centenary of the construction of the Church and a booklet, written by Rev. Moore was produced.

Numerous gifts to the church were donated over the years, the bell is the oldest and most interesting, dated 1678 and inscribed :

'The gift of Dame Mary Beaumont, eldest daughter of George Burdet, Esq. of Denby Hall'

The Bishops sanctuary chair was given by Miss M. Hinchcliffe, it is one of a pair, the other (larger and more elaborately carved) is in Wakefield Cathedral and bears the arms of the city of York and was the chair of the Lord Mayor of York in 1617.

Paintings on the pulpit are also worthy of mention, these were painted by the Cawthorne based artist Roddam Spencer-Stanhope. The pulpit has recently been restored to its original dark wooden finish after being painted a gaudy white colour for a time.

Finally the electric lighting was subscribed for by the parishioners of Denby, in memory of their Vicar, Rev Tibbits who died in 1939. Inside the Church there are two memorials of note. The first is in memory of Charles Kilner, a professor of music who died in 1858, the second is the war memorial, it contains the following names:

Names on the War Memorial in the Church

1914-1918:	*James Moore*	*Charles Edward Jelfs*
	Edwin Jackson	*Herbert Norton Jackson*
	John Ellis Broadhead	*Charles Kilner Barraclough*
	Noah Green	*Fred Firth*
	Thomas Hodge	*Arthur Williamson*
	Gladstone Beever	*George Clement Boothroyd*
	John Walshaw	*Joe Hirst*
	Charles Godfrey Hinchcliffe	*John Wright*
	Archie Roberts	*Keble Thomas Evenett*
	Henry Sheard	*Joseph Bottomley Rotherforth*
	Albert Jackson	*Frank Cook*
	John Cook	*Charles Ralph Douglas Bell*
1939-1945:	*Cyril Schofield*	*Ernest Roebuck*

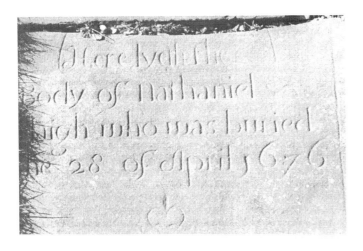

Above: The tombstone of Nathaniel Haigh.

Below: Rev. Sheard Circa 1940.

Above: Denby Churchyard in 1951 before the gravestones were removed.

Below: Denby Choir, circa 1935. Rev. Tibbits is at the far right on the third row.

Below: Job Johnson, Denby's First Vicar.

54

Denby was in the diocese of York until 1836 when it was transferred to the newly formed diocese of Ripon. Another new diocese was formed in 1888, that of Wakefield, and Denby was transferred here, under, whose jurisdiction it remains today.

The Parish registers begin as follows:

Baptisms - 12 January 1851 (before this date Denby baptisms were performed and recorded at Penistone)

Marriages - 22 February 1854

Burials - 2 January 1851 (though tombstones in the churchyard prove that in fact burials had been taking place here for some time. For instance, Nathaniel Haigh's tombstone is dated 28 April 1676, Mary Woolsind, 14 April 1723, Isabell Haigh, 20 December 1672.

William Couldwell died on 30th July 1783. His tombstone has a most interesting inscription, described as a clothier, the following transcription is almost complete, save for words which are illegible due to cracks and weathering:

> *"Frail is the vestment once I made,*
> *Death hath -?- this human thread,*
> *My frame I thought to firm so-?-,*
> *Was but a clothing for the soul,*
> *The cloth and thread I wove and spun,*
> *By time and weather were undone,*
> *The stronger texture of my frame,*
> *That web of nerves was just the same,*
> *And now the fates that spun the chain,*
> *Have cut the thread of life again."*

More modern times have seen the clearing of the stones from the front graveyard, sometime in the early sixties, because of its overgrown and generally poor condition. The stones were positioned all around the boundary walls of the churchyard where they remain today. I was informed by the late Mr. Jack Waldie that not a single complete gravestone had been taken away so genealogists need not despair.

In 1993, mainly due to vandalism, a number of gravestones and crosses were broken and desecrated, signifying the change in moral attitudes inherent in today's society when compared to our God fearing forbears. In 1990 Denby Dale became a separate parish leaving St. Johns at Denby and St. Nicholas's at Cumberworth to form a United Benefice. In 1994 a festival of flowers celebration was held inside the church and also in the school where an exhibition of village memorabilia was displayed. A commemorative plate was also commissioned.

Charles Broxholme	*1627-1635*	*John Brownhill*	*-*
Daniel Clarke	*1635-1643*	*Brice Bronwin*	*1830-*
- Miller	*-*	*Job Johnson*	*1851-1887*
John Crooke	*1657-1665*	*Alexander Barrington Orr*	*1887-1894*
Timothy Kent MA	*1665-1691*	*Romeo Edwin Taglis*	*1894-1926*
Gamialiel Battie	*-*	*Gervase Orton Tibbits*	*1926-1938*
William Norris	*1698-*	*Reginald Jackson Sheard*	*1939-1944*
Bryan Allot	*-*	*Norman Aubrey Moore*	*1944-1982*
Jonothan Perkins	*1729-*	*Norman Stanley Fox*	*1982-1984*
Samuel Phipps	*1751-1761*	*Robert Christopher Shaw*	*1985-1990*
Francis Haigh	*-*	*David James Clarkson*	*1991-Present*

QUAKERS

The movement begun by George Fox because of dissatisfaction with the normal form of worship probably arrived in High Flatts around the year 1652. When a person was converted (or 'convinced') he became a 'friend', of which a number belonged to the village of Denby:

John & Henry Dickinson (High Flatts), John Turner, Richard Priest and Thomas Crowder (Denby), John Swift and Arthur Brooksbank (Gunthwaite), John Blackley (Gunthwaite Hall) all belong to this 'Quaker Dawn' during the 1650's.

Whilst in its infancy the participants in the movement were persecuted for their beliefs. Acts were introduced to prevent meetings taking place, for not conforming with the established church, for not paying church tithes or swearing the Oath of Allegiance. For example, for being at a meeting in 1660, Richard Priest and John Marsden of Denby (amongst others), were imprisoned for three weeks. The term of imprisonment varied from days to years. In 1684 Joshua Green of Denby and Mathew Burdett of Nether Denby had been in prison for over two years for refusing to take the Oath of Allegiance. Burdett finally took the Oath and was released, Green remained in prison for some time. Refusing to pay church tithes also warranted severe punishment, John Crowder of Denby had his goods taken in kind on 13

Quaker Bottom, High Flatts. Present Day.

occasions between 1675 and 1683 valuing over £6. Crowder was a farmer and usually wheat, oats or barley were the items removed. The Quakers had a tradition for poor relief and charity work, not just within their own circles but in the 'outside world'. In 1826 an operation was mounted to help the people in the township of Denby. The problems in the village had been caused by the changes in the textile industry. At a meeting convened in May chaired by Elihu Dickinson, it was reported that in Denby there were 127 poor families, consisting of 664 individuals, this was roughly half the population of the village, of which 55 - wholly employed, 145 - partially employed, 208 - unemployed, 256 - children under ten years old.

The average earnings of these people was calculated to 1s 7.5d a week, the meeting resolved that a subscription should be raised to help.

As the movement grew and gained solidity, particular families and individuals gained in importance, The Dickinson's regularly turn up in records as not only staunch supporters of the movement but major landholders as we shall see later when we examine the Denby Enclosure Map of 1802. One other 'friend' from High Flatts worthy of note is Joseph Wood, a man of great character and an illustrious preacher and believer, his success and the records he left during his lifetime (1750-1821) are a testament to the ideal Quaker of his time. For more details on the Dickinson's and Joseph Wood see the book 'Plain Country Friends' by D Bower and J Knight. In 1764 there were eleven Quaker families living at Denby which met each Sunday (along with others numbering over 100), under Henry Dickinson at the 'Friends Meeting House' at High Flatts.

As we have already seen meetings traditionally began to take place here during the time of Oliver Cromwell's republic (1649-1660), these were in a barn on the site of the present meeting house. At the end of the 17th century a purpose built 'Meeting House' was erected and the graveyard was first used in 1790 (a smaller one at the front of the Meeting House was now full).

This hamlet at High Flatts was for many years populated by Quakers and became known as Quaker Bottom. At its peak High Flatts was probably one of the largest country meetings in this part of Yorkshire.

In 1886 a home or sanatorium was opened for 'the restoration of inebriate women of the working and middle classes' in Mill Bank House, built by Elihu Dickinson at High Flatts. This home for women was run by women. Due to the support of the 'Yorkshire Women's Christian Temperance Union' the home continued to run into the early years of the twentieth century. Inmates suffering from alcoholism were aided in keeping away from temptation, although shut away, many managed to kick their habit and indeed returned to help the inmates at the home after their own release. In 1901 the manageress was a Mrs Peace.

An interesting aside to the latter is the story that the 'George' public house is also reputed to have been a sanatorium running along similar lines before it became a tavern.

Today this sleepy hamlet is largely untouched by modern development, the cobbled paths, the stately meeting house and the ordered graveyard evoke memories of these Quakers of the past.

CHAPELS

A Wesleyan Reform chapel was built in 1911 (next to what was the Post Office until the 1990's), its life was short-lived being closed in 1930 and converted into a private dwelling by J W Heath.

A Zion chapel was built on Barnsley road in 1860 which proved popular, so much so that a new building was commissioned, completed in 1908. The roof and south gable of this newer building were severely damaged by high winds in 1962.

The chapel's community activities included the staging and performance of plays. The photograph overleaf gives a flavour of the type of costume worn for these.

Taken in front of the older chapel. A group of Amateur performers line up for the camera, circa 1923.

Today, congregations at most churches and chapels are dwindling, yet in the past these organisations were the pivotal supports of society around which everything was organised. Without them, village history would be much the poorer and although people today use them mainly to perform Christian ceremonies, and to celebrate major religious festivals, their loss would be a severe blow throughout the parish.

EDUCATION

The Schoolhouse, Lower Denby, circa 1895. Mrs. Challenger and her daughter lived in the first half of the house. The second half still retains the distinct appearance of a school although by this time it was uninhabitable.

The first detail we have concerning education, regards a donation made by William Turton of Denby. In 1443 he gave £3 9s 4d out of his lands to the school at Penistone.

Long before education was made compulsory a school was in operation in Lower Denby. According to the Victoria County History, Francis Burdet, of Denby Hall left £200 in his will, dated 24 June 1731 to provide for this and for the poor of the village. The sum was finally invested in 1769 in a cottage, barn and ten acres of land at Hoylandswaine. This site was let for £12.6s per annum, half of this sum was paid to the school master and the other half provided for six free places for local scholars.

The provision of education before 1870 was very much dependent upon religious efforts and voluntary bodies. For the working class children of Denby, Sunday schools, Charity schools and Dame schools were the options available. Along with the school at Lower Denby, there was also a boarding school run by Joseph Shaw at High Flatts from the mid eighteenth century. This was closed between 1877 and 1899 due to a fall in numbers. A Dame school was run from a house on Miller Hill in what is now Denby Dale (then Denby Dykeside). These were more common in the eighteenth century, usually run by an elderly woman, they provided a limited education for children before they reached an age when they became economically useful to their parents and prospective employers.

In 1849, the Denby vestry meeting decided to repair the school at Lower Denby. New shutters and doors were erected, being paid for by the poor rates. The 1851 census notes that David and Elizabeth Hoyle, both from Marsden were the Master and Mistress at this time. Owing to a decline in numbers the school was closed for 2 or 3 years before 1861. An attempt was made to revive it, but the building was old

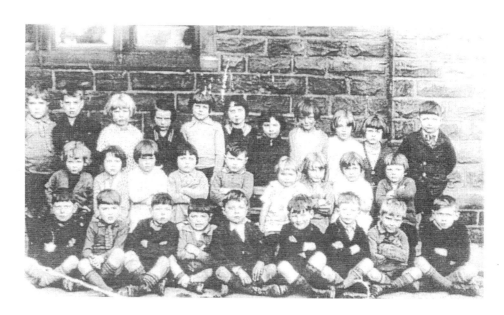

Denby School - 1934.

Back Row: *Terence Windle, Dennis Walshaw, Barbara Roebuck, Freda Knowles, Joyce Schofield, Winifred Jackson Betty Cartwright Joan Miller, Marjorie Walshaw, Ruth Jones, Donald Beldon.*

Middle Row: *Denise Dronsfield, Lucy Coburn, Zena Herbert, Betty Drew, George Jackson, Joan Hinchliffe, Audrey Dronsfield, Madge Roebuck Betty Roebuck.*

Front Row: *John White, Derrick Morris, Jack Thorpe, Harry Heath, Stanley Barber, John Stanley, Derek Greaves, Gordon Hinchliffe, Gordon Blacker.*

and now unfit for teaching purposes, this led to its final demise in 1876. The endowment (now lost) became applicable for a prize fund under a scheme dated 5 August 1880. The building was later converted into a private home and has now been enlarged, but one of the old round windows from the original property still remains and the name 'The Old Schoolhouse', survives on the wall to remind us of the establishment which was created long before the introduction of compulsory education.

In 1864 the Church day school was built at Denby for the education of all in the township. The land was given by Thomas Kaye of Bradford, the cost according to the 19th century trade directories was £750. The state became more involved with education from 1870 when an act was passed which paved the way for free and compulsory education by 1880. Children were required to attend school from the ages of 5 to 10 when providing they had reached a certain educational standard they would then be

Denby National Schoolchildren - 1872. The master behind them is probably Charles Hargreaves.

Upper Denby Boys, circa 1926

Denby Schoolchildren, dressed for a wedding party in May 1907

allowed to work part time whilst still attending school. The earliest Master I have been able to find is one Charles Hargreaves along with a schoolmistress, Miss Roberts. It is likely that he is the Master behind the cluster of children in the photo on the latter page, dated 1872, he was certainly the Master in 1881.

Scholars came from the surrounding villages of Denby Dykeside, Ingbirchworth, Lower Denby, High Flatts, Fray Royd and Broadstone to name a few. It is probable that the creation of this new state supported school, known as Denby National, helped signal the demise of the charity school in Lower Denby.

In 1877, 1 page of the register notes that there were 30 children attending, ages ranging from Harry Taylor who was 13 to Edith Haigh who was 4 years 6 months old. It can only be surmised that the Master and Mistress must have struggled with the differing levels of maturity within their classes. Though the standard of teaching at this time was basic, the three 'R's' and religious studies comprising much of the syllabus, and classes were regularly depleted because of truancy, which in many cases was brought about by parents keeping their sons and daughters away, to work and bring some money into the household.

The register also shows the previous schooling of a child. In many cases the answer was either none at all or that he or she was being re-admitted. There are though some interesting examples, such as James Taylor, whose family had moved from Manchester to Denby. His father was noted to be a labourer, why he had moved from the city where jobs were more commonplace to settle in Denby's quiet backwater will always remain a mystery, though it does seem a little odd.

A column entitled 'reasons for leaving' is also very illuminating: 'working full time under age', 'lives over two miles off', 'went to another school because I, (the Master, presumably Mr Hargreaves) wanted 10 school pence' and other variants on this theme.

It is also very interesting to note the occupations of some of the local fathers at this time :

Farmer, Joiner, Stonemason, Porter, Weaver, Collier, Saddler, Besom (Broom) Maker, Road Sur-

Taken at the front of the school, well before the construction of the present day porch. Mrs. Jelfs with her class circa 1924.

Denby schoolchidren prepare for May Day in 1959. Christine Martin is the May Queen.

veyor, Tailor, Delver, Publican, Coachman, Mechanic, Hawker, Gypsy, Gardener, Designer, Spinner, Railways, Grocer, Shoemaker and Policeman to name but a few.

It is possible that by 1885 a Mr Milnes had become the Master of the school, the register notes a Herbert Milnes who's father was a schoolmaster but although they lived in Denby it does not say where his father taught. Abel Jelfs became schoolmaster around the turn of the century, working alongside his wife and becoming very well known and respected throughout the village. Mr Jelfs had a seat on the Gunthwaite and Ingbirchworth Urban District Council in 1917 though he held other similar positions at other times.

It was Mr Jelfs who organised gardening classes across the road from where the Church gates stand today. Children would be sent to collect leaf mould from Swift Wood, which was used to fertilise the ground. These classes resulted in striking floral displays, which some of the older residents still remember today. These gardens were later turned into allotments, which are now buried under two new houses.

In 1928 a 'Sale of Work' booklet was produced, which contained quotations and recipes such as :

"One swallow does not make one summer; but one pin maliciously inserted in the bottom of a chair does certainly make one spring"!

This quote cane from Mrs J.Jelfs, although it is nice to see she had a sense of humour after learning that she used to have a stick that would reach from the front of the classroom to the back, enabling her to sort out troublemakers with the minimum of effort.

The Jelfs moved from Denby to Bromsgrove around 1930, Abel being followed as Master by a Mr Taylor. Subsequently Miss Close and Miss Thompson were to take over, names that will still be familiar to older residents. Miss Thompson lived in the schoolhouse which was connected to the school via a door and porch as did all the previous Masters or Head teachers.

In 1918 the school leaving age was raised to 14, almost dispensing with the school/work ethic after a child was 10 years old, this was followed by a division of schools with a transfer between tiers at the age of 11. In 1944 the leaving age was raised to 15 and free secondary education became available to all children at either, Grammar, Technical or Secondary Modern schools, selection for these was decided by the 11+ examination. Denby students moving on to either Penistone Grammar school or Skelmanthorpe Secondary Modern (now Scissett Middle School). In 1973 the leaving age was again changed, to 16 years old where the situation stands today.

Denby C of E school was under threat of closure during the 1980's, but has survived and is still a very important part of the township. Extensive refurbishment has been completed in the 1990's updating the building and creating a modern day village school, though externally the building has little changed. The long arched window, facing towards the common now extends to the floor of the playground and a porchway has been constructed at the main entrance. Though heavily reliant on fund raising ventures the school seems to have a secure future.

THE 19TH CENTURY

We are now into a century from which far more written records survive, enabling us to create a fuller picture of the inhabitants of the village and their occupations, which we will consider later.

We start in 1806 with the village militia. By this time the militia was largely voluntary and was never called upon to resist an invasion. It essentially balanced the standing army and aided in local politics. Of course the members of Denby's force could have been called upon at this time to dispel luddite activists but to date I have found no direct evidence to confirm this.

Militia for the Township of Denby.
First Class , (men under 30 having no children).

Name	Age	Occ.	Name	Age	Occ.
Armitage Isaac	21	weaver	Hanson Edward	24	weaver
Armitage Joshua	23	weaver	Hanson John	26	weaver
Barlow Joseph	21	weaver	Haywood Benjamin	19	weaver
Barraclough James	19	weaver	Haywood Thomas	22	weaver
Barraclough John	19	weaver	Helliwell Joseph	23	weaver
Beaumont Joshua	22	farmer	Horn William	18	weaver
Beaver Benjamin	19	servant	Hough John	21	cottonspinner
Bedford John	18	weaver	Hudson Benjamin	23	weaver
Bedford Joshua	21	weaver	Kaye James	19	weaver
Biltcliffe Amor	19	weaver	Kilner William	18	weaver
Blachell James	20	servant	Kirk John	19	weaver
Blackburn Amos	22	farmer	Langley Joseph	21	weaver
Boothroyd Benjamin	21	tailor	Lockwood Thomas	21	weaver
Brown Benjamin	18	weaver	Lummax Joseph	27	weaver
Brown Thomas	26	weaver	Mallinson George	19	cloth manufacturer
Brown William	21	weaver	Marsden Benjamin	21	weaver
Burdett Christopher	20	weaver	Marsden John	29	weaver
Burgess David	26	weaver	Marshall Francis	29	tanner
Burgess Francis	23	weaver	Mosley Benjamin	18	servant
Crowther James	18	weaver	Mosley Thomas	19	weaver
Crowther Jonas	20	weaver	Moxon Thomas	21	weaver
Dalton John	20	weaver	Pattrill (Irishman)	28	shoemaker
Dickinson Elihu	24	farmer	Revil George	28	weaver
Dickinson Jonothan	21	weaver	Revil Jonathan	18	tanner
Dickinson Joseph	19	weaver	Richardson Charles	24	weaver
Dickinson Richard	29	tanner	Sagar Joseph	20	weaver
Ellis John	27	cloth manufacturer	Shore John	28	weaver
Gaunt Joshua	19	labourer	Stephenson Jonathan	21	slubbin
Gaunt Miles	20	dress manufacturer	Thorp William	22	weaver
Gaunt William	27	drysalter	Tinsdale Joseph	22	weaver
Graham Joseph	27	servant	Tyas George	18	shoemaker
Green Edward	20	weaver	Walker Charles	20	servant
Green James	20	servant	Watson John	20	tanner

Green Joseph	28	labourer	White Amarous	23	servant
Haigh John	28	weaver	Willard Cornelius	20	weaver
Haigh Thomas	18	weaver	Wood Joshua	19	weaver
Hall Charles	19	weaver	Wordsworth John	20	weaver
Hammerton Henry	21	tailor			

Exemptions : Elihu Dickinson (tender eyes), Francis Marshall (lost an eye), John Marsden (knock knees).

Militia Second Class (men above 30 having no children).

Name	Age	Occ.	Name	Age	Occ.
Burdett William	35	weaver	Priest Joseph	33	cloth manufacturer
Ellis Thomas	33	cloth manufacturer	Robinson Benjamin	40	cloth manufacturer
Haigh James	30	farmer	Sagar James	35	cloth manufacturer
Haigh Thomas	37	farmer	Shaw Jonothan	38	cloth manufacturer
Marshall John	39	tanner	Taylor James	30	labourer
Marshall Michael	37	farmer	Tyas David	37	shoemaker
Mitchell Thomas	41	farmer	Tyas Jonothan	30	cloth manufacturer
Priest John	39	farmer	Wood William	40	cloth manufacturer

Exemption : Jonothan Tyas (substitution).

Militia Third Class (men between 18 and 45 having children but none under 14).
None.

Militia Fourth Class (men between 18 and 45 having children under 14).

Name	Age	Occupation	Name	Age	Occupation
Addy Thomas	25	weaver	Hinchcliffe Charles	43	cloth manufacturer
Beaumont William	23	weaver	Kilner Thomas	25	weaver
Biltcliffe George	29	weaver	Lockwood Joseph	30	weaver
Biltcliffe Mathew	24	weaver	Morton Simion	30	weaver
Broadhead George	24	weaver	Mosley Joshua	24	butcher
Corkhill William	26	weaver	Peace George	19	weaver
Dickinson Joseph	24	weaver	Robinson George	37	shoemaker
Ellis John	24	weaver	Rusby Samuel	40	butcher
Gartside Firth	29	dyer	Shaw Giles	31	cloth manufacturer
Gaunt Joshua	25	cloth manufacturer	Shaw Samuel	37	farmer
Grayson William	25	weaver	Tunnicliff Thomas	29	labourer

Appeals against the list were to be heard at 10am on the 17th September at the White Boar Inn, Barnsley. The list itself was compiled by John Shillitoe (Constable) and dated 12th September 1806.

The following year saw the freeholders of the township having to travel to York to vote in the great election, the names opposite can also be found in the above Militia list:

The Yorkshire Poll 5th June 1807.

The following people had to travel to from Denby to York to vote for either William Wilberforce, Henry Lascelles or Lord Milton:

			W	L	M
Barraclough	James	(Yeoman)			1
Burdet	William	(clothier)			1
Dalton	John	(clothmaker)			1
Dickinson	Henry	(clothier)			1
Dickinson	Elihu	(clothier)	1		1
Dickinson	Weightman	(miller)			1
Dyson	Daniel	(clothmaker)			1
Ellis	John	(clothier)			1
Firth	Jonothan	(farmer)			1
Gartside	Firth	(dyer)			1
Gaunt	Joseph	(farmer)			1
Graham	John	(innkeeper)			1
Haigh	Thomas	(Gent.)			1
Haigh	William	(farmer)			1
Haigh	John	(labourer)			1
Heywood	Christopher	(farmer)	1		1
Horn	Francis	(Yeoman)			1
Kendrew	William	(butcher)			1
Morley	Joshua	(butcher)			1
Parker	Thomas	(farmer)	1	1	
Revil	Jonothan	(clothier)			1
Robinson	William	(clothier)	1		
Senior	John	(husbandman)			1
Sleigh	Thomas	(clothier)			1
Wood	William	(manufacturer)			1
Wood	Joseph	(farmer)			1
			4	1	24

The election result overall was: Wilberforce 11808, Milton 11177, Lascelles 10000.

These 26 people represent the more affluent members of the village at this time, though the labourer John Haigh would seem out of place, perhaps he was a direct relative of the Thomas, noted as, Gent. It is also tempting to speculate that John Graham could have been the landlord of the Star Public House but this is undetermined.

What is most readily apparent are the amount of people involved in textile work, from manufacturers to weavers and this will be considered later.

Denby Workhouse

As the country's population continued to rise during the 18th and 19th centuries, many workhouses were built or converted from other buildings to house and employ a growing army of paupers. The following extract is taken from Dransfield's, 'History of Penistone' and concerns the one at Denby:

"Memorandum of Agreement made this 1st day of October 1827, at a meeting convened for that purpose between the inhabitants of Denby Township in the Parish of Penistone and the County of York on the one part, and Jonathan Shaw of the above written Township and County on the other part, viz:

The said Jonothan Shaw doth agree to take all paupers of the said Township into his house in form of workhouse upon the following terms, viz:

The rent, three pounds per year, to be paid half yearly by the overseer of the poor of the said Township. When wheat is under 25s per load the paupers maintenance to be 2s 9d per head, per week, and when 25s and under 35s per load the paupers maintenance to be 3s per head, per week, and 35s and upwards to be 3s 3d per head, per week, with the addition of 1s a week for coals. And at any time there should be no paupers within the said workhouse, deduct the 1s for coals. And the said inhabitants doth agree to the above statement and also to furnish the said workhouse with such bedsteads and bedding and other furniture as may be agreed upon by the said parties at this or any other time, and the said inhabitants doth also agree to furnish the said paupers with necessary clothing and paid for by the Overseer of the poor.

And the said parties doth agree to give each other three months notice in writing previous to the giving up of the said workhouse, and everything according to the inventory to be accounted for and given up peaceably and free from damage at the expiration of the three months notice. As witness our hands this 27th day October 1827."

Signed in the presence of - William Turton and John Gaunt by
Richard Mallinson (for John Mallinson) - Assistant Overseer.
Jonothan Shaw.

The following is an inventory of goods placed in the workhouse by Richard Mallinson, 27th October 1827:

2 bedsteads and cords, 2 beds with straw, 2 long pillows, 2 coverlids, 2 long pillow cases, 4 forks, 1 round table, 1 long pillow case, 1 twill tick bed and chaff, 3 sheets, 4 blankets, 1 tub, 3 stools, 4 knives, 3 spoons, 2 blankets (new), 1 coverlid (new).

Shaw's building was situated at the back of what is now the Southcroft housing estate, a little way down Gunthwaite Lane on the left and was part of a smallholding called Robinson Lathe. The remains which comprise a grass covered mound with odd stones poking out of it, are probably those of the workhouse though most of the site has gone forever. Robinson Lathe, possibly a property owned and named by a family called Robinson, and there are numerous mentions of such a family in this book, was an enclosure, inside which were a barn, outbuildings and a cluster of dwellings. It was in one of the old buildings that Denby Band was to practice before moving to the wooden hut further down the lane. One presumes that the workhouse, Shaw's residence, must have been the original farmhouse, as it had to be a building with a fair number of rooms.

In 1834 the Poor Law Commission queried the Overseers of the poor of Denby about the following particulars of the workhouse :

Q : State for what number of persons there is room in such poorhouse or workhouse or other houses, and also the greatest number which have been in the workhouse or other houses at any one time.

A : The premises occupied by the contractor for the reception and maintenance of the poor are pretty large and might accommodate twenty paupers. The greatest number that he has had at any time has been seven paupers.

A detail from 'Baines' - Trade Directory of Yorkshire dated 1822, lists some of the occupants of the village who could possibly have attended the meeting mentioned above, to inaugurate the workhouse:

Amos Barraclough (Star public house)
James Barraclough (Blacksmith)
John Bentley (Grocer & flour dealer)
John Wood & Sons (Fancy weavers)
Joseph Langley (Grocer)
Joseph Dalton (Corn miller)
Joshua Dyson (Grocer & draper)
Joshua Moxon (Miller)
Rev. John Brownhill (Vicar)
Ward & Haywood (Scribbling millers)
William Hague (Wagon&Horses)

The list is somewhat longer, though small compared to the total population of the township at this time, which was 1412, an amount recorded in the following table for 1821:

From the Victoria County History (VolumeIII).
Table of population, Penistone Parish:

Village	Acreage	1801	1811	1821	1831	1841	1851	1861	1871	1881	1891	1901
Whole	22773	3681	4231	5042	5201	5907	6302	7149	8110	9094	9482	11160
Denby	2885	1061	1132	1412	1295	1690	1709	1813	1637	1559	1661	1765
Gunthwaite	952	111	119	86	99	66	77	81	83	70	68	57
Hunshelf	2465	327	429	436	531	578	729	1150	1283	1404	1559	1680
Ingbirchworth	1105	170	264	367	371	419	393	368	303	335	321	274
Langsett	4914	204	235	325	320	303	296	280	246	271	263	922
Oxspring	1202	219	255	247	283	241	278	346	370	350	322	397
Penistone	1134	493	515	645	703	738	802	860	1549	2254	2553	3073
Thurlstone	8116	1096	1282	1524	1599	1872	2018	2251	2639	2851	2735	2992

The population expansion at Denby reached a peak in 1861 but remained fairly constant thereafter. It is interesting to note the dramatic upward trends of Langsett and in particular, Penistone. Until 1881 its population was less than that of Denby, yet due to the arrival of new industry, the total doubled between 1871 and 1901.

The 1851 Census

The census returns for the township of Denby list 1709 inhabitants though these include people from Birdsedge, Ingbirchworth, Denby Dale and many others. The returns list a persons address, fore and surname, marital status, age, occupation and birth place, enabling genealogists to flesh out the lives of their ancestors. The occupations make for interesting reading as does their frequency :

Domestic	34	Scholar	83	Woollen Engineer	1
Stone Mason	8	St Masons Lab	2	Stone Masons Son	1
Fancy Manufacturer	1	Farmers Wife	4	Fancy Weavers	102
Piecer	7	Miner/Collier	6	Woollen Dyer	1

Occupation	No.	Occupation	No.	Occupation	No.
Fulling Miller	8	Carder	3	Slubber	5
Fancy Finisher	2	Labourer	9	Bobbin Winder	37
Blacksmith	4	Bob.Wndr. Home	1	At Home	11
Blacksmith Assistant	2	Dressmaker	4	Road Labourer	6
Shawl Knitter	2	Railway Labourer	3	Agricultl.Lab	35
Plate Layer	3	Drawer	1	Washer Woman	1
Annuitant	1	Land Holder	4	Wool Willower	1
Farmers Son	4	Wife	4	Fancy Waistcoat Weaver	16
Cook	1	Shawl Knotter	1	Shoemaker	4
Tailors Son	1	Tailor	3	Teacher	3
Cotton Dyer	6	Cart Driver	2	Cordwainer	4
Woollen Weaver	3	Invalid	1	Warper	3
Visitor	2	Carpenter	4	Carpenter Assistant	2
Carpenters Wife	2	Farmers Daughter	2	Carpenters Son	1
Power Loom Weaver	7	Errand Boy/Girl	8	Winder	1
Beer Seller	1	Twist Winder	1	Glazier	1
Plumber/Glazier	2	Cropper	2	Dress/Bonnet Maker	3
Collector Ric.	1	SKRV	1	Bakery	1
Nurse	1	Prop. Herbs	1	Handloom Weaver	2
Rag Sorter	4	Pauper	4	Landlord	5
Rtd. Farmer	3	Burler	3	Visitor Sawmill	1
Shopkeeper	3	Builders Son	1	Tailor & Inn	1
Building Master	1	Worsted Dyer	3	Warehouse Man	1
Corn Miller	1	Governess	1	Inn & Shop	1
Farmer	31	Farmers Son	4	Gas Maker	1
Pattern weaver	1	Butcher	1	Laundress	1
Woolcomber	1	Saddler	1	Woollen Spinner	1
Whiskey Maker	1	Shawl Fringer	2	Washer Woman	2
Mechanic	1	Stone Gritter	1	Machine Joiner	1
Steam Loom Weaver	1				

Again, as we have already noted, much of the work in the township was textile oriented, add to this the farming community and its dependants and only domestic suppliers and workers remain, with the odd exception.

It is also interesting to note the numbers of people living in places which still exist today, for instance

Surname of family and number of people on Ratten Row, 1851: Beaumont 3, Blacker 2, Boothroyd 2, Gaunt 6, Hanwell 12, Hirst 2, Lees 2, Moors 2, Morton 3, Newsome 3, Senior 2, Wood 2, Barraclough 1, Burdett 1, Moore 4, Robinson 1, Weetman 2, Horton 1, (51 people).

Surname of family and number of people at Denby Hall, 1851: Gaunt 7, Haigh 1, Lockwood 11, Mayon 1, Lockwood 10, and servants, Armitage, Askey, Fenwick, Mahon, and Whitaker, (35 people). (NB: two separate Lockwood families).

Trade Directories

The trade directories of the 19th and early 20th centuries were similar to the telephone books of today, of course without the telephone numbers as Alexander Graham Bell didn't patent his machine until 1876!

They supply a few short details concerning the history and geography of the village and the names of all the noteworthy persons who lived and traded there. The earliest one I have discovered for Denby, is, as we have already seen dated 1822. Others exist in local libraries for the years; 1838, 1857, 1861, 1866, 1867, 1881, 1889, 1901, 1904, 1912 and 1917 though there are likely to be a few others.

These directories enable us to follow the progression of family business's and their subsequent transferrals of ownership or closure, the following are extracts taken from the directories up to the beginning of the 20th century :

White's Directory 1838 (Vol. 2).

George Houldon	(Gent)	Joseph Turton	(Schoolmaster)
Thomas Turton	(Surgeon)	Thomas Whitehead	(Schoolmaster)
George Wiley	(Registrar)	Jas. Barraclough	(Blacksmith)
Joshua Shaw	(Blacksmith)		

Post Office Directory   - Yorkshire 1857.

Private Residents:

Herbert Cam Dickinson Esq.		Miss Dickinson
Mrs Mary Firth	Mrs Hunter	
Rev.Job Johnson MA	George Norton Esq.	
Thomas Turton Esq.	John Wilkinson Esq.	

Commercial:

Thomas Turton	(Surgeon)	James Armitage	(Farmer,Coal Owner)
Elihu Barraclough	(Blacksmith)	Benjamin Boothroyd	(Tailor,Tanner)
Francis Burdett	(Shopkpr&Joiner)	Joshua Dyson	(Farmer)
John Ellis	(Stonemason)	John Gaunt	(Farmer)
George Firth	(Chairmaker)	Aaron Hanwell	(Shoemaker)
Joseph Haigh	(Farmer)	John Milnes	(Wheelwright)
George Micklethwaite	(Shopkeeper)	George Norton	(Quarry Owner)
Miles Moore	(Stonemason)	George Tyas	(Shopkeeper)
Thomas Shillitoe	(Farmer)		

Whites Directory 1866:

Francis Burdett	(Joiner)
William Laundon	(Saddler)
John Wood	(Tillage Merchant)
John Wood & Charles Homes (Corn Millers)	
John Hargreave & Co.	(Coal Owners)
Thomas Turton	(Surgeon)

Kelly's Directory 1881:

Joseph Barraclough	(Blacksmith)	Ellen Barraclough	(Farmer)
Henry Boothroyd	(Tailor)	John Boothroyd	(Taylor)
James Burdet	(Shopkeeper)	Francis Burdet	(Shopkeeper/Joiner)
Gideon Dixon	(Farmer,Hall)	Thomas Ellis	(Clerk to Local Board)
Charles Hargreaves	(Nat.Schoolmaster)	George Micklethwaite	(Shopkeeper)

John Hargreaves	(Farmer, Upper Bagden)	James Moore	(Stonemason)
John Kilner	(Shopkeeper)	James Slater	(Farmer)
Joseph Milnes	(Farmer)		
William Priest	(Farmer)		
John Turton	(Chemist)		

Kelly's Directory 1889:

Aaron Wood	(Farmer, Denby Hall)	Joseph Barraclough	(Blacksmith)
Martha Barraclough	(Shopkeeper)	Charles Bedford & Son	(Rope Manufac.)
Henry Boothroyd	(Tailor)	James Burdet	(Shopkeeper)
Mark Gaunt	(Farmer)	Henry Haigh	(Farmer-Tenters)
Alfred Thorpe	(Farmer, Fall Edge)	John Turton	(Surgeon)
John Heath	(Wheelwright)	John Horn	(Farmer)
Henry Lockwood	(Farmer, Denby Hall)	Arthur Priest	(Farmer, Shopkpr)
John Micklethwaite	(Quarry Owner, Farmer, Post Office)		
Charles K Hanwell	(Collector to Local Board)		

Kelly's Directory 1901:

Lord Saville - Lord of the Manor.

Post Office - John Micklethwaite (Sub postmaster)

Council meetings take place in council room at Denby Dale on the 2nd Thursday in the month at 7pm.
Members: Chairman - Thomas Norton JP DL
Vice Chairman - John Hinchcliffe
Clerk - Wilfred Barns of Denby Dale
Treasurer - Frederick Crawshaw of Penistone
Medical Officer of Health - Duncan Alistair McGregor of Clayton
Surveyor - Charles Hinchcliffe of Denby Dale
Sanitary Inspector - George William Moxon of Denby Dale
Abel Jelfs is schoolmaster (max. kids at school 200 - average att.140).

Delarever Burdet	(Farmer, Denby Common)	James Burdet	(Shopkeeper)
William Challengor	(Blacksmith)	Henry Firth	(Farmer)
Aaron Hanwell	(Shoemaker)	Harry Heath	(Wheelwright)
Elizabeth Lockwood	(Threshing Machine Owner)		
Turton Turton	(Farmer, Fall Edge)		

The latter listings are only representative samples and yet they supply the names of the people and families involved in the different occupations considered later in the book.

Local Government

Until 1895 the administration of Denby was in the hands of the vestry which was mainly concerned with roads and the poor. Their records were preserved in a Town Chest, a fact noted by historian W.H. Senior who discovered a record from 1849 ordering the chest to be repaired and 'three locks and keys provided for three rate payers to hold'.

The Denby and Cumberworth Urban District Council was created in 1895. This body remained until further reorganisation took place in 1938 when the four old councils were united to form the Denby Dale

Urban District Council. The council was divided into four wards, those of, Emley, Skelmanthorpe, Clayton and Cumberworth & Denby Dale.

The Denby Dale Urban District Council was finally absorbed into the new borough of Kirklees in 1974.

Turnpike Roads

Used by traffic including, stagecoaches, wagons and carts the turnpikes were roads maintained by tolls collected from travellers. By the 1830's there were more than 20,000 miles resulting in tolls in excess of £1.5 million annually, though 80% of the nations roads were not subject to this system. The introduction of the railways led to the dissolving of the turnpike trusts due to the significantly reduced traffic and responsibility for the roads was transferred to local authorities.

A few years before 1810, John Metcalfe of Knaresborough constructed two miles of road over Birdsedge and High Flatts being paid £340, these new roads began to replace the old dirt tracks, preparing the way for today's road network.

John Metcalfe, or 'blind Jack' as he was known was born in 1717 and lost his sight at the age of four, he was a military musician, playing troops into battle at Falkirk in 1745, where he was taken prisoner. He made his name as a builder of houses, roads and bridges and it is reputed that he made the trans Pennine road from Huddersfield to Manchester. He died aged 93 in 1810.

William H. Senior noted that, the Denby vestry held a meeting in 1845 to consider the proposal to build a turnpike from Barnsley to Shepley Lane Head. They decided to oppose it in Parliament with the help of the Barnsley Canal Co. and to meet legal costs from the highway rate, unfortunately, for them, they were defeated and the road went ahead. By 1850 there were three turnpikes running along the boundaries of Denby and Cumberworth and although tolls were collected a significant amount of Parish funds were required to maintain them.

The Parish Council road surveying team in Gunthwaite circa 1910. On the far right of the wagon is Sam Burdet, a member of the family which were once Lords of the Manor.

Railways

The first sod for the Huddersfield and Sheffield Junction line was cut by Lord Wharncliffe at Penistone in 1845. Its construction was very labour intensive as many tunnels, embankments, cuttings and viaducts. were necessary. The first viaduct at Denby Dale was completed in 1847, though this first wooden structure was replaced by a stone one between the years 1877 and 1879, the line being officially re-opened in 1880. In Denby the hollow known as the 'basin' was dug out and sledged into Denby Dale to provide filler for this new viaduct. By 1850 the Lancashire to Yorkshire railway extension was opened and more routes followed throughout the decade, as rail travel opened up opportunity's never before considered by village people.

New industry began to arrive and flourish, mills which needed to be near water for power were built in the valley below Denby and the foundation of the modern village of Denby Dale took place.

Gradually, due to the effects of the growing road transport system some of the least used lines were closed. During the 1930's until after the second world war new investment was at a minimum until nationalisation in 1947 but the line which runs through Denby has long been in danger of closure.

HANSON & TURTON,
Photographers, DENBY DALE.

Street Lighting

W. H Senior noted in the book 'A History of Denby Dale Urban District Council' that the Denby board maintained street lighting for the Denby Dale Gas Co., though for more rural areas oil lamps were provided. Acetylene gas replaced these in 1904, invented by R J Moss & Sons of Birmingham. It is also interesting to note that the picture on the front of their advertising leaflet was drawn from a photograph, of William Challenger, lighting one of these lamps in Lower Denby, around where the telephone box currently stands.

Town gas was piped from the works in Denby Dale to Denby by the early 20th century, indeed the author's own Great Aunt and her brother were responsible at one time for going round the village, ladder in hand, in order to light them.

William Challenger seen at Lower Denby posing for an advertisement for Moss & Sons, inventors of an Acetylene gas lighting system.

Water & Sanitation

Details, again supplied by W.H. Senior tell us that an outbreak of cholera in 1849 left the district with serious problems over sanitation. Not until 1878 was a medical officer appointed for Denby and Cumberworth. Duncan McGregor was paid £30 per annum by the Denby board and only £11 by Clayton, his first report on the area was very critical.

Doorless privies, defective drains, bad odours, no sink drains (so water ran across gardens, and people emptied chamber pots onto the roads)! Measures were put into place to rectify these problems, though by 1895 only 20 new privy's had been built and 20 sinks trapped. A bye-law of 1898 forbade any householder to shake their rugs or mats or to empty chamber pots on the roads.

Mr. Senior also noted that the Denby vestry minute books before 1871 record permission to sink wells for water by the villagers. Unfortunately by 1875, many of these had become contaminated by water from Zacheus Hinchliffe's colliery. The wells were eventually abandoned after agreement had been reached with the Dewsbury waterboard to supply to the village.

Before we continue on into the 20th century we will now examine in a little more detail some of the trades and occupations adopted by the Denby villagers during the 19th and early 20th centuries, to try and flesh out and explain much of what has been discussed in this chapter. Small rural villages were generally self supporting, but many of the practices and skills familiar to our ancestors have either changed beyond recognition or become obsolete and many of their workplaces have now been destroyed or modernised changing the face of the village forever.

PUBLIC HOUSES

From late medieval times the public house has been a part of English culture. Three basic types existed at this time:

Inns	-	usually providing meals, and accommodation,
Taverns	-	for 'respectable drinking',
Alehouses	-	for the general public and commoners.

It was during the 16th century, after the growth of Protestantism had curbed Church centred social drinking that 'Pubs' became more a part of everyone's everyday life. Figures suggest that there was one alehouse for every 150 people by 1577.

The modern Public house began to emerge during the 19th century. Apart from their sign these alehouses looked very much like private homes. As literacy spread and became more common place the name of the pub was added to the sign, and also the brewers name began to be shown.

There were originally three 'alehouses' in the modern village of Upper Denby, namely the Star, New Inn and the George, and two more at Lower Denby, the Wagon and Horses and the Dunkirk or Junction.

The Star, which was adjacent to the buildings that were to become the George, was certainly operating by 1822 when we find Amos Barraclough as the landlord.

In 1830 duty on beer was abolished by Parliament which meant that any ratepayer could then sell it for consumption on or off his own premises without a licence. Around 1838 the New Inn began trading, being followed by the George, around 1857. Free trade in ale was brought to an end in 1869 opening the way for a gradual extension of ownership of pubs by the breweries. This led to a number of closures, particularly during the years 1899 - 1904 when an act was passed which raised a levy on the whole licensing trade to provide some compensation for publicans who had lost their licenses.

The licensing act of 1872 gave magistrates the powers to grant licenses and check for the adulteration of alcoholic drinks, they also fixed closing time at 11.00pm. Licensed victuallers thought these too excessive whereas temperance societies conversely thought them too lenient.

The public bar was originally in the kitchen of an Alehouse, which would have had a partitioned off area known as the taproom. More discerning customers used the parlour or best room. It was only when kitchens became private that the public bar was called the tap room. By the 1850's there were three grades of rooms, the bar room (standing), the tap room (sitting), and the parlour or best room. During 1845 because of the repeal of duties on glass the bottling of beer became practicable and signalled the decline of pewter tankards which were finally replaced by glasses towards the end of the century.

The George and the land around it was owned by the Norton's group up until 1877 when it was bought from their trustees. In 1882 it was noted by the Barnsley Permanent Building Society that the pub was owned by Reuben and James Senior and that the property comprised a barn, carthouse, garden, carriage house and one cottage and that it was occupied by George Taylor. Before its history as a pub the building which became the George was used as a sanatorium, presumably upon similar lines to the one at High Flatts as we have already noted. The building, which is recorded on the Enclosure map of 1802 is probably of 18th century origin and was originally a small farmstead.

Seth Senior and Sons brewery began trading in 1829, the story goes that Seth borrowed a sovereign to begin brewing in his own cottage and became so successful he was able to start the business, where he was joined by his sons, Reuben and James. They took over many pubs around the Shepley area, including the 'Sovereign' named as a reminder of their humble beginnings. They became owners of both the George and New Inn at Denby and although not in existence at the pubs origins they were also to take over the

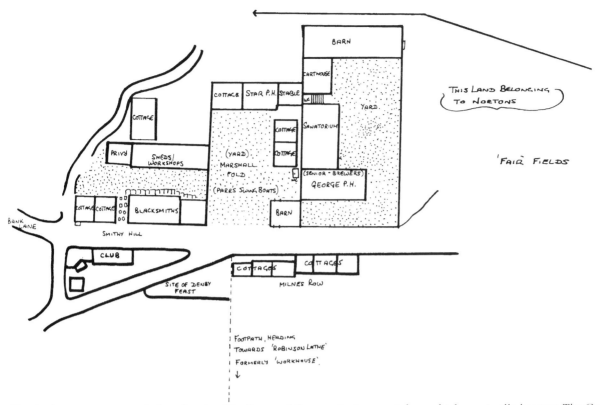

The Authors reconstructed plan showing The Star and the sanatorium next door which eventually became The George.

Star. On 21st November 1946 Seniors were taken over by Hammonds brewery of Lockwood which signalled the demise of their name in pub ownership.

The Star's days were numbered when the George, next door to it, began trading. In its last year or two should any customer require a drink of beer it had to be hurriedly fetched in jugs from the George, after which it was poured straight into glazed pots, complaints about its quality were rare as no one could see whether it was clear or not! It closed around 1904 probably as a result of the compensation made available by parliament. The landlord, Joshua Swainson, went on to take over the Dunkirk at Lower Denby and the building was converted to a private residence by J.W.Heath and Mr Town, the pub sign lying in the old Heath joiners shop for many years.

The New Inn and Ratten Row, circa 1910.

Denby Footballers in front of The George, circa 1909.

IN THE WEST RIDING OF THE COUNTY OF YORK.

PETTY SESSIONAL DIVISION OF STAINCROSS.

LICENSING (CONSOLIDATION) ACT, 1910.

At the Transfer Sessions holden at the Court House in Barnsley on the
fourth day of **August** 19 **26** for the Division of
Staincross in the West Riding of the County of York.

The Licensing Justices for the said Division hereby grant to

George Henry Buckley ————————————————

of   6 Barnsley Road, Darton ————————————————

this Justices' licence authorising h im in substitution for   Edward Daniels

———————————————— who holds ~~(or has held)~~ a licence in
respect of the premises mentioned below to hold an excise licence to sell by retail
at the licensed premises situated at   Denby ————————————————
in the said West Riding, known by the sign of the   "George Inn"

———————————————— any intoxicating liquor which may be sold under
a spirit-retailer's or publican's licence for consumption either on or off the
premises ~~an excise licence to sell beer by retail for consumption either on or~~
~~off the premises.~~ ————————————————

This licence shall be in force from this day until the Fifth day of April next.
Witness our hands

The licence held by George Buckley for The George 1926.

76

Year	The Star	The New Inn	The George
1822	Amos Barraclough		
1830	ThomasBurdet		
1838	John Firth	John Brook	
1857	John Firth	John Hanwell	Enoch Taylor
1861	John Firth	John Hanwell	Enoch Taylor
1866	Aaron Hanwell	John Hanwell	Enoch Taylor
1867	Aaron Hanwell	John Hanwell	
1881	Aaron Hanwell	Mary Hanwell	Nancy Taylor
1882			George Taylor
1889	Aaron Hanwell	Mary Hanwell	George Taylor
1901	Wilson Green	Hannah Pearce	Alfred Taylor
1904	Joshua Swainson CLOSED	Harry Thorpe	Alfred Taylor
1909			Joseph Airton
1912		Sam Wing	
1917		Sam Wing	Benjamin Slater
1926			Edward Daniel
1927		Percy Cartwirght	Genny Buckley
1930		Percy Cartwright	Frank Widdowson
1950(app.)		Walt Martin	Frank Widdowson
1952(app.)		Eric & Joyce Bailey	Frank Widdowson
1954		Doug & June Fisher	Frank Widdowson
1958		? Fisher	Frank Widdowson
1959		? Fisher	Jim & Dot Barber
1963		CLOSED	Jim & Dot Barber
1971			Roy Barraclough
1992			Martin & Carol Brook
1993 - Present			Steven & Jill Slater

N.B. It should be noted that the dates given are not terms of tenancy but the years known in which the pub was occupied by that person.

These pubs were very much different from today's comfortably furnished affairs and ran slightly differently. The floors were either wooden or simply stone flags. A fire would blaze behind the hearth and customers would be served at their tables by the landlord after attracting his attention by rapping their pots on the table or ringing bells at the back of their seats. Beer was simply a pint of best or mild, customers often asking for a 'gill of ale', which was supplied in either pewter, or later glazed, pots. These were places for drinking and talking, not for eating and listening to music.

The landlords, usually, ran their pubs alongside their other jobs, ie:

John Firth (Star) was also a shopkeeper and farmer, John Hanwell (New Inn), was a cobbler as was his kinsman, Aaron Hanwell (Star) and Joseph Airton (George) was a plasterer, a fact which he advertised on the sign for his pub.

During the 1950's the New Inn was a popular place for a drink, particularly with local farmers. Other than the best and mild brews offered by Hammonds one could also partake of bottles such as: Guards Bitter, Prize Medal or perhaps Town Major. Smiths crisps were sold out of tins of 18. The New Inn also offered funeral teas, unlike the George at this time. The upstairs room would be used for such occasions, a room which was at this time apparently full of stuffed birds! The steps to the cellar were so badly worn into the shape of a barrel that one unlucky customer, perhaps the worse for drink? fell down them, much to the amusement of the attendant clientele.

A customer walking in would see the best room on the right and the tap room to the left, the bar was straight in front and only the width of the hallway, the privies were outside, round the back. Entertainment was sparten, but on occasions a village lady, Ginny Grange, would gain a free glass of beer to take home providing she sang to the accompaniment of the piano for the landlady. The pub had a darts team which played in the Penistone league and the landlady would sometimes offer round steak teacakes as a snack.

In 1963 the New Inn closed down. Hammonds had decided that one of its two pubs in Denby should be modernised and the other closed. The George had the advantage as it already possessed a car park. The brewery approached the owners of the land across from the New Inn, with a view to building one, but were refused permission the decision was therefore made for them and the house was sold and converted into a private residence.

The Dunkirk/Junction at Lower Denby was operating from at least 1866 when we find Elizabeth Burgess as the landlady, giving way the following year to Allen Booth. The present building was originally three cottages, the early pub being run from one of them. These were purchased by the Cubley brewery of Penistone in 1887 and were knocked through to create the building we have today.

The Wagon and Horses across the road was also an early alehouse. In 1822 the landlord was a William Hague, he was followed by 1838-Joshua Shaw, 1861-Mrs Senior, 1867-John Johnson (to at least 1881). From at least 1901 - 1912, William Challengor ran a blacksmiths shop at the side of the pub.

Only the George remained in Upper Denby, the barn and carthouse were demolished to extend the car park and a new toilet block was added.

The spittoon's were given by the landlord, Jim Barber, to a farmer at the bottom of Cuckstool in Denby Dale to use as pig bowls. The pub still retains its traditional village character having its busiest times around Christmas, particularly Boxing Day, when the Rockwood Harriers meet in the car park and crowds of traditionalists turn up to watch them depart before entering the pub, usually frozen cold and ready for a pint.

WHEELWRIGHTS, JOINERS & UNDERTAKERS

The Wheelwright

The masters of this skill were very important to the local farming community, sometimes they worked in tandem with the village blacksmith in a job which involved both wood and metal.

The nave or naff was turned on a treadle lathe (the one from Denby was donated to the Tolson Museum, Huddersfield), and great precision was required to fit the spokes and felloes (rim). Hard woods were used, though cast iron naves began to appear from 1846. Once the wooden parts were assembled the metal tyre was added with the aid of a tyring plate. The tyre was red hot when forced onto the rim and then drenched to shrink it tight around the wheel.

The carts and wagons they were made for varied locally throughout the country. Carts were two wheeled, wagons four wheeled. The dray seems to have been a popular type for Denby farmers being low and strong and suitable for heavy goods.

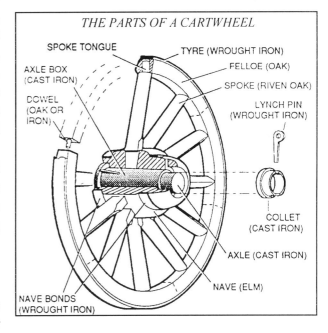

THE PARTS OF A CARTWHEEL

SPOKE TONGUE
TYRE (WROUGHT IRON)
AXLE BOX (CAST IRON)
FELLOE (OAK)
SPOKE (RIVEN OAK)
DOWEL (OAK OR IRON)
LYNCH PIN (WROUGHT IRON)
COLLET (CAST IRON)
AXLE (CAST IRON)
NAVE (ELM)
NAVE BONDS (WROUGHT IRON)

Denby Wheelwright's and Joiners

John Milnes was the Denby wheelwright in the 1851 census, where he can be found employing four men and two grandsons. His premises were reputed to be in the building at the end of back lane, now coal pit lane, just a little way from the Barraclough blacksmiths shop.

He was a member of a large family of farmers, his relations working at both Broad Oak, Gunthwaite Gate and Oughtibridge Hall farms.

His grandson, John Heath from Oughtibridge, became one of his apprentices in the late 1840's and was then set on as a full time employee after his apprenticeship ended. In 1868 John Milnes died, aged 88, it is likely that he had already passed much of his business over to his grandson by this time, but it was now that John Heath inherited sole responsibility. He was also responsible for burying his own grandfather as the business involved undertaking, though it was unusual for a family to bury its own. He was laid to rest in Denby Churchyard free of charge, usual cost £2. John married Ellen Hanwell and had a large family, his sons, Walter, Rufus, John Milnes and Harry all became joiners and wheelwright's, and aided in the family business.

Before the introduction of stone for buildings, timber was the chief source material. The people that built these wooden structures were known as 'wrights'. The Latin word for 'wright' is 'carpentarius', therefore makers of wheels were wheelwright's, more general woodworkers were carpenters. On the other hand, joiners were involved in the construction of furniture only, which led to friction between them and the carpenters. Today the two terms are interchangeable but originally they were two different professions.

John Milnes and the Heath family had no such reservations and wore all three different hats, alongside other maintenance work such as glazing and painting and repairs to just about anything.

The following list will illustrate this and also the prices charged and the clients they worked for:

John Heath's Ledger, 1882 onwards:

Name	Work Undertaken	Cost		
Sarah Gaunt	Close Post		1s	
Wilson Green	Child's Coffin		3s	
Denby Local Board	Mattock Shaft			10d
	Barrow Repaired			10d
David Tyas	New Cartwheel	£2	5s	
	New Cart Axle		16s	6d
John Micklethwaite	Manger Repaired			9d
Arthur Priest	Short Ladder			9d
James Moore	New Gate		18s	
John Boothroyd	New Book Case	£1		
	Chest of Drawers	£4	10s	
George Schofield	Pig Sty Door & Hanging		11s	6d
Joseph Barraclough	New Stool		2s	6d
(blacksmith)	Shoeing Box Repaired			6d
	Pattern Making		6s	9d
Benjamin Holmes	Cart Wheel Rimming & 5 spokes	£3	3s	
	Cart Bottom Repaired			8d
Zion Chapel	4 New Doors, Hanging & Locks	£1	2s	3d
Aaron Hanwell (shoemaker)	Last Tops Making		1s	6d
John Kilner	Little Pig Trough		4s	
	Spout Putting Up & Painting		10s	6d
	Table Repaired		1s	4d
Mary Hanwell (New Inn)	Billiard Cush Putting On			6d
	Chair, new rockers		1s	9d
James Burdett	2 shelves, putting up		2s	9d
William Fretwell	Wheels rimming & 4 new spokes	£1	8s	3d
Tom Thackra	New Hawking Cart, springs, fittings, iron work etc.	£17	0	0
John Horn	Turnip Chopper repaired		3s	9d
	Plough repaired		6s	9d
John Haigh	Dray undergear repaired		8s	10d
Rev. Job Johnson	Pegy repaired			4d
	Cupboards for Church		9s	
Denby School Manageress	New Desks & Floor rests	£1	18s	6d
	School floor repaired	£1	12s	
	Class room boarding	£3	17s	
	Desk top removing & planing		3s	9d
John Burdett	Cart painting & varnishing		17s	6d
George William Moxon	New Dresser	£4	15s	
Charles Rusby	Cart wheel rimming		17s	
Alfred Gaunt	New cart axle		17s	
Erasmus Smithson	New Dray Wheel	£1	17s	
Church Work	New Belfry Floor	£4	11s	6d
Church Work	New seat in gallery		2s	4d
	Steeple Roof Repaired		8s	9d

When Died	When Buried	Name	Age	Price
1858				
December 5	Dec 8	Joseph Gaunt	68 years	1 6 0
Dec 11	Dec 14	Nancy Crosland		Stuff 3 6
Dec 17	Dec 20	Thomas Wood	90	13 6
			24 do	extra 4 9
Dec 18	Dec 22	Amelia Crosland	30 do	1 7 / 13 6 / extra 4 9
1859				
Jan 30	Feb 1	Shaw Crosland	8 Months	4 6
May 16	May 20			4 6
Aug 24		Henry Ridal	10 Months	extra 2 6
Aug 29	Sep 1	Reuben Morton	19 years	1 0 0
Sep 26	Sep 29	William Walter Beever	11 Months	0 7 6
Oct 29	Nov 1	Hannah Morton	59 years	1 0 0
1860				
Feb 23	Feb 26	Mary Wrontin Morton	89 years	13 6 / extra 5 6
July 20	July 21	Mary Taylor	1 Month	4 6
July 27	July 29	Ann Wood	14 years	1 4 0
Dec 4	Dec 6	Martha Henley	2 weeks	0 2 6
Dec 4	Dec 7	Richard Milner	35 years	2 4 0
		Cickhill Child		0 2 6
1861				
Jan 15	Jan 20	Emma Hinchliff	20 years	1 6 0
March 18	March 22	Joseph Birchell	25 do	0 14 0 / extra 5 6
April 7	April 11	Susannah Birchell	16 do	14 0 / extra 5 6
April 23	April 26	Lydia Whitaker	67 do	1 0 0
May 14	May 17	Mary Birchell	13 do	0 14 0 / extra 5 6
May 26	June 2	John Lockwood	21 do	1 4 0
July 9	July 13	Elizabeth Hirst	28 do	extra 14 6 / extra 5 6
Sep 14	Sep 14	Child at Clien Taylors		2 9
Oct 2	Oct 5	William Mann	56 years	0 15 10 / extra 5 6
Nov 5	Nov 8	Ann Lockwood	84 do	0 14 0 / extra 5 0
Nov 7	Nov 9	Edmond Greaves	12 do	0 14 0
1862				
Jan 5	Jan 8	Martha Hudson	50 do	0 14 0 / extra 5 0
Feb 9	Feb 12	Joseph Lockwood	87 do	0 14 0 / extra 5
March 29	March 30	Mary Little		1 0 0

The first page of John Heaths funeral ledger.

Work was also carried out for Zacheus Hinchliffe and Augustus William Saville to name but two, and clients came not only from Denby. but also Denby Dale, Cumberworth, Gunthwaite and others. The ledger is very long as is the above representative list, but it gives details about the everyday things in villagers lives as well as the financial aspects of woodworking. Of course, even in those days it could be difficult to recoup an overdue debt, ie:

No. 23, p. 214.—Notice of Service of Default Summons.

Barnsley Ct
No. of Plaint, 0249

In the County Court of Yorkshire, holden at Rotherham.

Between   John Heath   Plaintiff,

and

Henry Brooke   Defendant.

You are hereby informed that the Defendant was on the 24th day of May 1887, served with the Summons issued in this Action.

Dated this 25 day of May 1887

F. PARKER RHODES.

Registrar acting as High Bailiff.

To the Plaintiff.

Hours of Attendance at the Office of the Registrar, in Westgate, Rotherham, from Ten till Four, except on Saturdays, when the Office will be Closed at One o'Clock.

A summons taken out by John Heath to recover money owed by Henry Brooke, 1887.

Undertaking

A ledger has survived dating from 1858 detailing burials undertaken by John Milnes and John Heath. The price of a burial, as now, was varied. A child's burial would be around 5-9s, an adult burial anything from £1 10s and upwards depending on the type of coffin requested and arrangements required. Pitch pine was the cheapest material for these and is consequently the most used. As the ledger moves forward in years so the prices increase, ie: Rachel Fish was buried on Nov. 24th 1873 at a cost of £3 17s 6d. It is interesting to note that the linings for the coffins were accounted for in the ledger as '4 ½ yards of black stuff'!

The following breakdown shows the cost of the expenses involved in a burial on April 23rd, 1870:

John Burgess :

6½ yards of black stuff	4s	4d
Dress and Hearse	7s	6d
Grave Digging	12s	
Vault Wall & Stone Line	13s	

Minister charge for vault		6s	8d	
Dues at Church		3s	6d	
Total	£2	7s	0d	

added to the above was the charge made for the coffin which brought the total up to £2 12s.

By the early 1880's John's third son Harry was working alongside him as his partner. The close proximity of the workshop to the Barraclough blacksmiths probably aided in the union between the two families when Harry married Elizabeth Barraclough, daughter of the blacksmith, Joseph. Thus two integral village business's were drawn together. Two cottages which used to stand on Smithy Hill, next door to the blacksmiths were the homes for the two families. The houses, demolished in 1972 were of 17th century origin.

Cottages now demolished. on Smithy Hill circa 1965.

John Heath died in 1903 aged 73 in one of these cottages and Harry was left to carry on. Two of his children, Joe Willie and Ernest were to become joiners themselves, Joe Willie taking over the business after Harry's death in 1922 aged 59.

Joseph Barraclough died in 1907 and the buildings and land belonging to him were sold to Harry Heath. Presumably it was now that the joiners shop moved from the end of Back Lane into the outbuildings at the back of the blacksmiths on Smithy Hill, though it is likely, in view of the family union that the two sites were interchangeable.

Joe Willie Heath bought land across from the new site and constructed the present day Joiners shop in 1926, today this wooden structure has quite obviously seen better days, though plans were made at one time to rebuild in stone. His son Harry took over the business after working alongside him for many years, in 1969 after Joe Willie's death. Ill health and the reduced demand for traditional craftsmanship have all but seen the end of this family business, yet the advent of modern power tools and the 'do it yourself' enthusiasts will never take the place of these craftsmen of the past.

Joe Willie Heath his wife Harriet and family circa 1913.

Genealogical Table of the Milnes and Heath families.

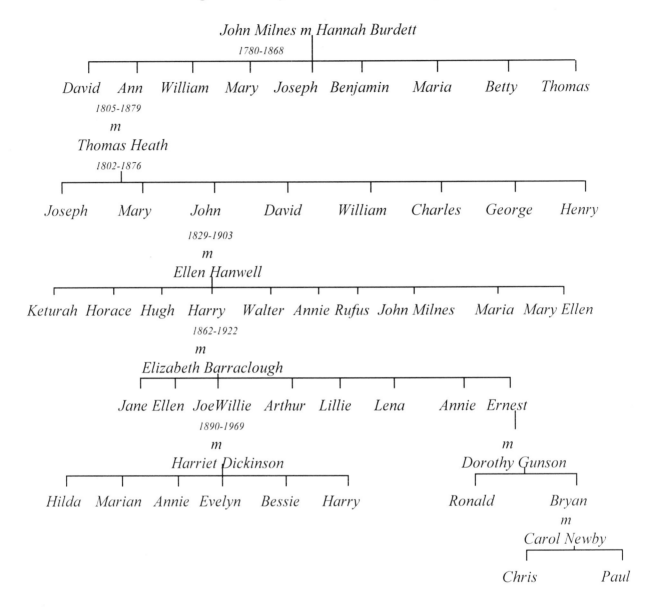

John Milnes m Hannah Burdett

1780-1868

David   Ann   William   Mary   Joseph   Benjamin   Maria   Betty   Thomas

1805-1879

m

Thomas Heath

1802-1876

Joseph   Mary   John   David   William   Charles   George   Henry

1829-1903

m

Ellen Hanwell

Keturah   Horace   Hugh   Harry   Walter   Annie   Rufus   John Milnes   Maria   Mary Ellen

1862-1922

m

Elizabeth Barraclough

Jane Ellen   JoeWillie   Arthur   Lillie   Lena   Annie   Ernest

1890-1969

m   m

Harriet Dickinson   Dorothy Gunson

Hilda   Marian   Annie   Evelyn   Bessie   Harry   Ronald   Bryan

m

Carol Newby

Chris   Paul

BLACKSMITHS

It was reputedly, the year 1600 when James Barraclough opened a Blacksmiths shop in Upper Denby. It is likely that this first building was just a timber structure, which later gave way to a brick built building which was only demolished in the early twentieth century. It stood on Smithy Hill, (not on the green as reported in the book; 'A Stroll Around Denbi'), and was not accessed from the front, but through an alleyway, between itself and the two adjacent cottages and round to the back, where there was also a joiners shop and at one time, a gin-race.

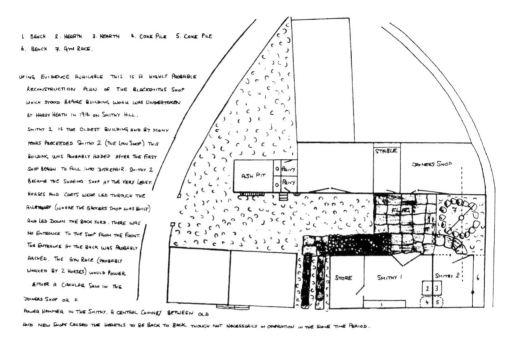

Reconstructed plan of the Blacksmiths premises in Upper Denby, circa 1880.

The Barraclough's continued to be the village blacksmiths until 1907, when the last of them, Joseph, died.

Many times employed in tandem with wheelwright's, the blacksmith was an important part of farming life, a myriad of tasks kept him busy throughout the hours of daylight.

The following abridged description is taken from 'Comptons Encyclopaedia Vol.3:'

The glow of the forge, the ringing clang of hammer against anvil, the sizzle of heated iron or steel cooled suddenly in water, and the neigh and stamp of horses were familiar sights and sounds in the shop, as the blacksmith repaired and made carriages, wagons, tools and machinery. Smithing is one of the oldest crafts and became increasingly important with the discovery of iron. In time it was discovered that heated metal could be shaped more easily. Time and experience brought skill to the arts of refining, shaping and tempering iron and steel.

Very few Blacksmiths shops exist today, there are fewer horses to shoe, wagons and carriages have given way to trucks and cars and tools and parts are now mass produced by machines. Tool and die making shops, rolling and forging mills and the steel industry in general have left little for the blacksmith to do other than the farriers task of shoeing horses.

Until well into the 20th century the community blacksmiths shop was a familiar sight. School children

The village blacksmith, shoeing horses, possibly at Lower Denby, circa 1895.

on their way home would peer through the open door into the dark, smoky interior. A leather approned smith might be thrusting tongs into the forge and pulling out pieces of white hot metal. He would turn quickly to the anvil, put the pieces together and hammer them hard to weld and shape them. Of course the shop was also a gathering place where farmers and others would muse over the problems of the day. The floor space in the shop had to be large, so as to allow the wagons, ploughs and horses enough space to be worked on. A workbench, water tub, anvil, tool table and coal bin would reside against the walls, as well as racks to hold metal rods and sheets used as raw material by the smith. The floor around the forge and anvil would have been either, packed soil or wood covered by sheet iron so that the chips of hot metal that flew when being pounded would not set fire to the floor. The anvil was usually placed about 6 feet from the forge and was made of steel, its face being hardened. It stood on a block of wood which was sunk into the ground to a depth of about 2 feet. The tongs a smith would have used varied in shapes and sizes and the jaws were of various kinds, being designed to hold different shapes of metal. For heavier work the smith would swing sledge hammers of varying weights. Other instruments were hot and cold chisels (for cutting hot or cold iron), and shaped instruments called, flatters, sets, fullers and swages, used for flattening or forming special shapes in the metal.

Although none now remain the Barraclough's once populated the township of Denby in enormous numbers, as one would expect for a family that had lived here for 300 years or more.

In 1851 we find James and Elihu both working at their trade, employing two younger members of their families as apprentices, Francis, aged 16 and William aged 13. James and Elihu's father James was also a blacksmith, and it seems to be through this line that the business was handed down. That Elihu was deaf and dumb seems to have been no barrier to him practising his skill. Other members of the family were employed in the textile industry and farming and butchery, though it is probable that some of them had a knowledge of some aspects of smithing. The humble family business, expanded over the years, and incorporated a shop in Denby Dale (where the present hardware store belonging to Marsden's now stands) and a shop at Lower Denby, which was taken over by William Challengor. It would seem that Elihu ran the Upper Denby shop, whilst James looked after Lower Denby and that the Denby Dale site was taken over some time in the late nineteenth century.

It was James's son, Joseph who inherited the business, trained by his father and uncle he was the last of a long line in Denby. His will, dated 1907, nominates his son George (also a blacksmith) and his son in law, Harry Heath as executors. Arrangements were made to sell the blacksmiths shop in Denby Dale, to Harry's brother, Walter Heath. The shop in Upper Denby was adjacent to Harry's own home, and was

Above: Using a tyring plate to apply a metal wheel rim, Cawthorne, circa 1892.

Right: William and Fanny Challenger, circa 1896.

bought by him, and demolished shortly after by Allot and Bedford of Denby Dale. The site was re-developed at a cost of £100.10s during 1911/12. As Harry was the village carpenter and undertaker, the outbuildings at the back of the shop, which included a joiners shop, continued to be used for many years more until these too were demolished.

The shop at Lower Denby had been taken over by William Challenger, around 1893/4. Married to Fanny Challenger, nee Robinson, the family had moved from Dakinbrook to the old schoolhouse in Lower Denby to allow William to work at the forge which used to be part of the buildings which comprised the Wagon and Horses public house.

His ledger began in 1894 with a Mr Thomas Fish of Foal Foot. Other clients included the Laycock's of Gunthwaite Hall, Charles Harley of Denby Hall, Erasmus Smithson of Nether End and the Denby and Cumberworth Urban District Council. From his ledger we are able to learn a little of the prices charged and the jobs undertaken by the smith at the time:

Pony, 2 shoes	1s	4d
Mare, 4 shoes	3s	
Brake handle for a cart.	1s	
Horse, 4 removes	1s	6d
Cart wheel bearing	1s	
2 cold chisels		2d
Key engine wheel	1s	

1 Mattock			1d
1 lock staple and 1 sprained door.			4d
1 dozen studs and putting in.			10d
1 mattock & shafting (a mattock was a kind of pick axe.)			4d
Repair machine blade.		1s	
Foal, 1 remove and foot dressing.		1s	
Pair of new plough traces.		3s	2d
1 shovel,sharpening			6d
1 muck fork, repaired			3d
1 hammer repaired			4d
1 coulter laid			10d

(a coulter was the iron cutter in front of a ploughshare).

The majority of the work was undertaken on behalf of the local farmers, and shoeing horses was by far and away the most common activity of the week. Finally it would be useful to note that although most of the accounts were eventually paid, a bartering or contra account system was still very much alive as W. H. Senior discovered on the page for Mr Cyrus Laycock of Gunthwaite Hall whose bill was made out for £1.6s.7d. He supplied Mr Challenger with pork and pooling fat to the value of 7s.7.d to be deducted from his bill which was settled in Feb. 1902.

Genealogical Table of Denby Barracloughs

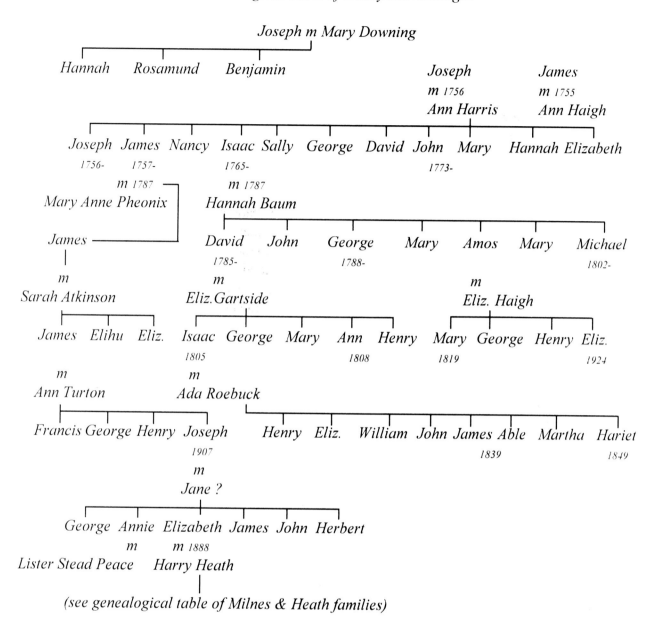

FARMING & TEXTILES

Farming

The art of living off the land is as old as the human race itself, its evolution would take far too long to tell in the context of this book and therefore we will concern ourselves with just the major points, applicable to Denby.

Denby's high elevation and the weather expected in this northern part of England meant that arable farming was never an important part of agriculture in the district. Of course crops were grown, but not on the same scale as those in more southern areas. Livestock became an integral part of life for many inhabitants of the village, sheep in particular, which could graze an the roughest pastures, led to the enormous boom which affected the village at the height of the cottage textile industry.

Crops, cattle and sheep amidst old fields and scattered farmsteads would just about describe Denby during medieval times. Within the fields, villagers would have their own strips of land, fairly proportioned to ensure that each had a fair share of good and bad. The results of the harvest would have been paid in part to Lord Burdet for his allowing them to farm on his land, a system known as 'feudal tenure'.

The black death of 1349, followed by other epidemics wiped out over a third of the population of the countryside in England, which led to a shortage of labour to farm the land, undermining the power of the manorial Lords. The peasantry became able to resist feudal obligations and feudal tenure was gradually replaced by rent.

By the late 17th century, agriculture had become an industry rather than a way of life. Manorial Lords had almost ceased to be farmers and were now landholders with tenant farmers, the peasantry were earning wages and subsistence economy was gone.

Due to a significant increase in population during the 18th century land became a good investment and ownership led to a steady increase in enclosure, which culminated in the enclosure awards made by the government at the turn of the century.

The Enclosure Award

Villages had been dividing up their open field systems long before the Enclosure Act was passed by parliament. The larger freeholders gained the biggest allotments, leaving the smaller, cottage farmers, who previously grazed their livestock on the common ground with much less acreage. Miles of dry stone walls sprang up creating a uniformity to the countryside and also paving the way for many of the roads we know today. Land that could not be ploughed or farmed was known as waste and was left for sheep to graze on.

The map which accompanies Denby's enclosure award dates from 1802 and a brief read through the names of the landholders soon provides the names of the more affluent members of the village. William Bosville held much of the land around what is now the present site of Upper Denby, he along with William Marshall, Charles Kent, Richard Lumley Saville and the Dickinson's of High Flatts are most prominent. Joshua Mosley held the lands around Manor farm, John Ellis held lands close to the Pinfold and William Kilner those that adjoined the chapel. Penistone Grammar school also had two plots at Lower Denby.

The plan on the following page, illustrates not only the owners of the property in the direct vicinity of Upper Denby, but also details the structures built before or during that time. It may be conjectured that here we have our earliest village plan, of buildings which must have been built in the 1700's and before:

The enclosure award book, which accompanies the map, details each landholders property by number, and also states their responsibility for its upkeep. It was checked on 18th November 1850 by George Wilby, George Rusby, Joseph Haigh, William Thorp, Jas. Peace and Herbert Cam Dickinson.

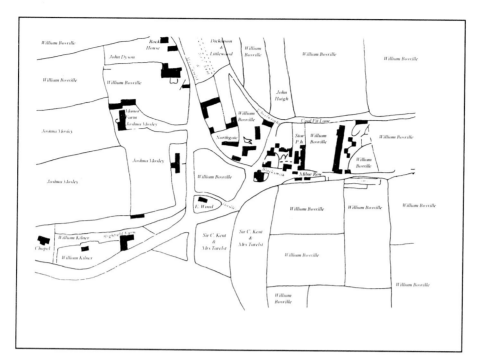

The Enclosure Award for Denby and Clayton was passed in 1800 and made on June 14th 1804. The plan is taken from the map which accompanied it, dated 1802.

Agricultural Revolution

Loosely dated 1750 - 1850 the revolution occurred because of the demands made upon farming by a rapid and constant increase in the population of the country. Ways had to be sought to increase productivity. The hand tools which had been used up to now were inadequate and labour intensive and it was a natural progression that the advances in technology should be applied to agriculture. Some of the more important innovations were:

1701	-	Jethro Tull's seed drill
1730	-	The Rotherham plough (wood and iron)
1770	-	The first all iron plough
1780's	-	Patrick Bell's reaping machine (pushed)
1784	-	Alexander Meikle's threshing and winnowing machines worked by a horse gin, later combined. Winnowing involved separating chaff from grain
1790's	-	Iron plough with replaceable parts
1802	-	Richard Trevithics first agricultural steam engine (to drive a threshing machine)
1840	-	Steam applied to cropping, crushing, threshing and winnowing
1888	-	Petrol engines
1902	-	Ivel tractor, the Fordson selling 6000 in 1917 and by 1956, 478,000
1920's	-	Combine harvesters (developed fully in the 1950's)

The development of the latter gradually caused bitter resentment amongst the labourers who feared the loss of their jobs or reduced wages. The appearance of the threshing machine, coupled with steam power led to acts of arson and animal mutilation by some labourers in efforts to save their livelihoods. Though no records survive for this in Denby it is certain that feelings ran high.

Power

Oxen were used from the earliest times being followed from at least the 12th century by horses. Stationary machines, housed in buildings were worked by either horse gins or water power where available.

Steam power became widespread during the 19th century, both for static machines and ploughing and cultivating with the use of traction engines until it was superseded by around 1914.

The 20th century has been dominated by petrol and diesel and by electricity for static machinery and dairying.

Threshing machine being used by the Pickford family probably at Gate Farm around 1920. Threshing was usually a communal effort. A group of neighbouring farmers would help each other on their farms utilising the one threshing machine available. Sheaves were fed into the top with the husks coming out at one end and the grain at the other. Besides the hard work in keeping up to the machine it was a dirty and very dusty job -particularly at the husk end. There was also a high risk of fire when using a traction engine to power the thresher.

Traction engine at Gate Farm with Clem Pickford aboard it, circa 1920.

Ploughing the old fashioned way. The Picture was taken in a field beloning to Gate Farm. The Pickford family first came to this farm in 1912, therefore the photo must have been taken soon after.

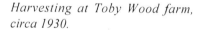

Harvesting at Toby Wood farm, circa 1930.

The Corn Law Act, 1815

Innumerable acts have been passed by parliaments which have affected the farming industry but perhaps the resolution determined in 1815 is one of the more famous. During the Napoleonic Wars imports of corn from abroad had virtually ceased and British farmers had been encouraged to grow as much as possible to make up the shortfall. At the end of the war the fear was that a sudden surge of foreign corn flooding the markets would reduce the price and ruin the farmers. The above mentioned act was introduced to prevent any imports of corn until the British price had reached 80s per quarter. Although the act protected the farmers, bread prices were very high at a time when bread was the staple diet of the poorer classes. This became a symbol of the oppression of the poor until the acts repeal in 1846 under Peel's government. As many will know, in Denby Dale a pie was baked to celebrate the occasion, but enough has already been written of this.

Netherend and Manor Farm Barns

These two farms are almost opposite each other on the Barnsley road heading to Cawthorne just past Lower Denby. Manor farm, on the left has a barn which is dated to 1657, although it is possible that some of the other buildings in the enclosure are even older, possibly back into the 16th century and contemporary with the massive barn at Gunthwaite.

The walls of the old cruck barn at Netherend on the the right hand side of the road were, according to the gable end, built in 1663. Although there is evidence to suggest that this date on the lintel is inaccurate, it is again likely that a structure was sited on this land in the mid 16th century.

Lifestyle

Denby's rich pastures have always lent themselves to cattle farming. Not only for their meat, one wonders what these farmers of the past would have made of BSE?, but also dairying. For instance in the 1930's the cows would be fed on kale and turnip and supplied with buckets of water to drink from. Milked by hand using the traditional three legged stool the milk would be transferred from the bucket into a churn and put into a cooler before being bottled the next morning and taken out to customers. Nearly every farm would have had a milk round at this time. Once returned the bottles were washed in a large trough using a simple bottle brush.

Horses were kept to pull ploughs, work gins and tow carts and wagons and were frequently the prized animals on the farm. Pigs, hens, geese and suchlike would be housed in a traditional style farmyard adjacent to the owners lodgings.

It was regularly the job of the farmers wife to take care of the needs of these animals, feeding them and collecting eggs from the hens etc. Some farms made their own cheese and butter and along with any surplus eggs these would be taken to the local market, at Penistone to be sold to supplement the households income.

Fields were fertilised with natural substances, cow, pig and horse manure alongside the contents of human privies which were thrown onto the fields ready to be ploughed in. I have been told that the fields which are now South Croft were regularly covered in human excrement! Although sanitary conditions improved rapidly in the latter part of the 19th century, animal waste was and still is used to a great extent, even after the introduction of chemical fertilisers just after the second world war. Indeed not only is this method cheaper, it is also in line with today's growing demand for organically produced vegetables.

Farming has essentially changed little compared to other industries over the years. The methods of achieving results have encompassed technological developments but memories of the past can still be found today. Potato picking for instance is still done by hand and other jobs such as dry stone walling can never, it would seem, be done by machines.

Male members of the Sykes Family in front of Manor Farm Cottage, circa 1910.

Textiles

By the 18th century woollen and worsted fabrics were the dominant industries found in West Yorkshire although cotton production was expanding rapidly. Throughout this time handloom weaving and domestic production was an important feature of the industry. Many of the occupants of the scattered upland farms of Denby combined weaving with smallholding, ie: Tenterhouse Farm, Manor Farm and Toby Wood Farm.

The shift to factory based production began around 1760, as hand labour was gradually superseded by steam powered machinery, though a glance through the 1851 census for Denby illustrates that domestic productivity in the village was as plentiful as ever.

The clothiers houses in upland districts, could, with steam power, become mills or factories. The fulling mills in the valleys became at first scribbling then spinning mills. In the latter part of the 19th century merchant manufacturers began bringing the different departments into one powered mill.

The advent of machines such as Hargreaves Spinning Jenny (1776), Arkwrights Carding Engine (1780) and Cromptons Mule (1779), led to serious opposition from domestic workers, of which the group known as the 'Luddites' are the most famous.

As the 'Luddites' believed, this new technology signalled the beginning of the end for domestic based spinning and weaving, though a brief respite did occur from around 1825 after the introduction of fancy weaving, which included the making of waist coatings, cords and sarsenets from materials such as wool, worsted, cotton and silk.

The 1851 census for Denby illustrates the growth of these industries within the village where we find:

102 Fancy Weavers and 16 Fancy Waistcoat Manufacturers, indeed a high proportion of the villages population were employed in some aspects of textile production.

Many of the textile oriented occupations listed have now become obsolete and their titles archaic, the following is an explanation of some of them:

Piecer	-	a person employed in a spinning factory to join together broken threads.
Carder	-	a card was an instrument for combing wool before spinning, a more strenuous occupation generally performed by young men.
Slubber	-	a person who twisted the wool after carding to prepare it for spinning.
Spinning	-	performed on a spinning wheel, normally by a woman, using a treadle which drove either one or two spindles, the process drew out and twisted the wool into threads.
Burler	-	a person who picked out knots in thread or wool in finishing.
Bobbin Winder	-	a person who used reels or spools to wind up the finished yarns.
Wool Willower	-	a person who worked a machine in which a spiked cylinder loosened or cleaned cloth, wool or rags for paper.
Warper	-	a person involved with stretching threads out length ways on a loom to be crossed by a woof, woof is thread for a weft. Weft are threads woven into and crossing the warp carried by a shuttle on a loom.

Once a piece of cloth was completed it then had to be sent for fulling, a process involving scouring or beating as a means of finishing or cleansing woollens, to thicken it. After shearing (or cropping) where the superfluous nap was cut from the cloth it was then tentered. Tenterhouse farm in Lower Denby survives to remind us of the frame, housed in one of the barns, which was used to stretch the cloth whilst drying, in order to keep its shape. Finally the piece would be dyed and then sold.

By the mid 19th century three mills had begun operating down in the valley at Denby Dykeside. Z. Hinchliffe & Sons began in 1850, J. Kenyon and Sons began in 1854 and Brownhill & Scatchard began in 1868. Gradually the occupants of the village of Denby drifted away from home based spinning and weaving to work in these factories, bringing with them their ready knowledge of the industry to these sites which had a plentiful supply of water for power.

By the early 20th century few of Denby's once large textile oriented population worked from home and the factories became powerful employers. The accident book of John Brownhill & Co. (formerly Brownhill & Scatchard), illustrates that the mills were on occasion dangerous places to work:

1926 - Eric Fretwell -   fractured right arm, caught in pulley wheel while oiling cropping machine.

1931 - Nellie Travis -   hit on forehead by shuttle.

1936 - Arnold Wood -   bruised head and wrist dislocated or broken, because of breaking of gantry while erecting jacquard.

1939 - Lena Heath -   hit by shuttle, slight injury to face, caused by breaking of spring on little picking stick.

Today only one of the three above mentioned mills is still running, that of Z. Hinchliffe, the demise of the industry signalling another change in the occupations of the populace of Denby.

Although there were craftsman and specialists in Denby from the earliest times the bulk of the population were originally employed on the land, as either farmers or labourers. Their adoption of the woollen industry steadily grew more widespread until its golden years in the 19th century. As technology progressed many of the men, women and children involved lost their jobs and were left at the mercy of the poor rates to support themselves and their large families. As we have seen, the Quakers of High Flatts mounted a charity operation to help the poor of Denby in 1826, poor because of the changes brought about in the textile industry. The coming of the mills in Denby Dale did create many jobs, but their decline, particularly in the latter part of the 20th century has left the area with no specific product to associate with the villages within it.

Many of the old farm buildings have now been modernised and turned into new homes for the changing community and the factory's in the valley are now largely retail units and warehousing space for new smaller company's, yet the woollen industry will always be associated with this part of Yorkshire and enough relics exist of that time to remind us what an important part it played in the lives of the ordinary people.

OTHER OCCUPATIONS

Denby Post Office

The Post Office, which was founded in 1635 grew steadily throughout the 17th and 18th centuries until the modern service blossomed, when parliament led by Rowland Hilder introduced the penny post in 1840. Telegraph companies were nationalised in 1870 when they were taken under the wing of the Post Office. A telephone was a regular feature of the shops after 1890.

Hannah Wood ran the nearest Post Office to Denby, in Denby Dale during the 1860's. Letters from Huddersfield would arrive at 7.30am and 5.30pm, they were despatched at 7.05pm. Hannah Wood had given way to John Micklethwaite by 1901. John was also a quarry owner and other members of his family ran a shop in Upper Denby during the last half of the 19th century.

The first Post Office in Denby itself was opened on 11th March 1914 by Harry Heath, the village carpenter. He had already opened a grocers store in 1907 and so the two were merged. His family continued to run the enterprise after his death in 1922, first Elizabeth his wife who was then followed, in 1947 by her daughter, Annie. Annie retired in 1958, aged 60, thus the Post Office was closed down, within two years the shop was also discontinued.

Being only a sub post office, services such as savings were not available, but the shop did possess a telephone in the 'corner' allocated to postal services.

Kathleen Wickam was the last proprietor of a sub-post office in Denby, also combining postal activities with a general store, this being closed in the 1990's, and so leaving Denby once again dependent on the sub - post office in Denby Dale for its services.

Shops

A glance through the trade directories of the 19th century provides the names of quite a number of people in this manner of business. For instance in 1881, James and Francis Burdett ran a shop, Francis was also a joiner, though it is possible that the shop was at High Flatts and not in Denby. John Kilner, and George Micklethwaite were also described as shopkeepers. The villages self sufficiency becomes even more apparent when one considers the farm produce available, particularly dairy items, the services of John Turton a chemist and the numerous cobblers, joiners, smiths, tailors and masons living in Denby.

Denby's General Store - 1904 to 1960

Harry Heath opened his shop around 1904 in a small structure, recently built between the Barraclough blacksmiths shop and two adjacent cottages, the building sited on the former alleyway through to the blacksmiths workshops round the back. As we have seen, he set up a Post Office here in 1914. His first ledger survives and this can be used to illustrate not only the price of goods in the period 1904-1915, but also to show the type of goods available at the time :

Boots and Shoes.

Clogs	2s	6d	Child's Slippers	1s	11d
Slippers	2s	6d	Men's Boots	8s	9d
Leather Lace Boots	6s		Canvas Shoes	3s	3d
Boys Button Boots	7s	11d	Ladies Boots	7s	9d
Tan, Strap Shoes	4s	11d	Sandals	3s	11d

Food Stuffs.

Bacolite Lard		3d	Onions		2 ½d
Flour (2 stones)	2s	10d	Ham		5d
Rabbit		11d	Marmalade		4d
Butter	1s	3d	Pepper		1 ½d
Potatoes		3 ½d	Salmon		8 ½d
Vinegar		1d	Mustard		1d
Tomatoes		6d	Bacon		4d
Candles		5d	Nutmeg		½d
Matches		2d	Oranges		3d
Eggs (½ dozen)		2d	Sago		3d
Tea		8 ½d	Beef		7 ½d
Treacle		5 ½d	Tongue	1s	2d
Tobacco (Bacco)		1 ½d	Ammonia		1d
Oatmeal		4 ½d	Blacklead		1d
Biscuits		3d	Jellies		2d
Rice		2 ½d	Beef paste		1d
Currants		4 ½d	Magnesia		2d
Sugar		4 ½d	Figs		4 ½d
Coffee		2 ½d	Soda		2d
Yeast		5d	½ stone of wheat	1s	5d
Apples		3d	Cheese	1s	2d
Jam		8 ½d	Cocoa		1 ½d
Camphorated Oil		2d			

Hardware and Fabrics.

Stockings	1s	3d	6 pieces of paper	1s	5d
Brush		4½d	Collar		4 ½d
Floor Cloth		2d	Shawl	6s	6d
Laces		1 ½d	Blouse	2s	6d
Needles		1d	Pair of Towels	1s	7d
Garters		2d	Blankets	3s	6d
Paint		6d	Scarf		5 ½d
Hairpins		½d	Broom	1s	
Apron		9 ½d	Hand Bag	1s	
Emery Paper		1d	2 pairs of Bloomers	5s	
Soap		2 ½d	Men's trousers	8s	
Starch		1d	Men's braces	1s	
Rope		1d	2 night dresses	9s	6d
Buttons		1d	A Child's Doll	4s	6d
Pins		1d	Box of chocolates	2s	3d
Comb		3 ½d	Corsets	5s	3d
2 Men's Shirts	2s	2d	2 men's vests	7s	6d
2 pairs of knickers	2s	4d	Smock	6s	6d
Teapot		6d			

(NB: it should be remembered that foodstuffs were sold in old weights and measures and the above are only representative samples.)

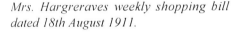

Above: Annie Heath with an unknown merchant, circa 1925.
Below: Delivery van above the cottages on Smithy Hill, circa 1935.

Mrs. Hargreraves weekly shopping bill dated 18th August 1911.

Note the absence of some of the foodstuffs that today we expect to find on supermarket shelves, bread, cakes, soup etc. These, of course all being made at home. Coffee beans were bought and ground down on the premises with the use of a grinding machine powered by an engine, previously owned by Norman Peace. The silver paper linings of the chests that tea arrived in were used for Christmas trimmings .

A license had to be obtained to sell fireworks for November 5th, Annie making sure that as many children as possible received a bag full with their name on it, usually more bangers for boys and snow-storms for girls The names 'Little Demon' , 'Thunderflash' and 'Jumping Cracker' evoke smoky memories of delighted faces. Toys were also sold although the store was definitely not a toy shop. In the early days stock was transported to the shop in a horse and cart later delivery's were made by company vans.

There were numerous other shops locally, notably that of Lucy Travis in Lower Denby which ran upon similar lines to the Heath one described above. A number of people also sold produce from their homes, vegetables, salad and other home grown items, and sweets, usually sold off a trestle table in the kitchen.

The Co. Op.
Founded in Rochdale the Co.Op grew steadily bigger from around 1844. The one in Denby was sited on Ratten Row and is still apparent, though now converted into a private dwelling, by the large front window, formerly the shop window. During the 1940's and 50's it was run by Teddy Higson. The big supermarket chains began to take over during the 1970's signalling the end of many Co. Op outlets and indeed village shops. The Co.Op closed in 1963.

Besom Making
This was the art of making brooms from twigs which were tied to handles, typical of the stereotyped witches broomstick.

The White family were responsible for this craft in Denby during the 19th and early 20th centuries. Fred White retired in 1923, after following in the footsteps of his father, Charles and his grandfather, John. The Besom's were sold to a number of sources, notably farmers and industrial factories.

Fred White had liberty to collect heather twigs on Honley Moor, Boardhill, Cannon Hall Park and all the moors around Denby. He used small oak poles, torn into thin strips to tie the heather to the poles, these were known as lappings. A report in the Huddersfield Examiner dated 1936 commemorated his golden wedding and he was quoted as saying:

"I once made one (a besom) for a sovereign in three minutes and it was another besom maker who bet me I couldn't do it. I had got my seventh lapping on when he was doing his second. Its grasp that you need in besom making, for holding the heather and tying the lappings round."

The White workshop used to stand as an outbuilding which backed onto Northgate, a usual weeks output was 10 dozen besoms.

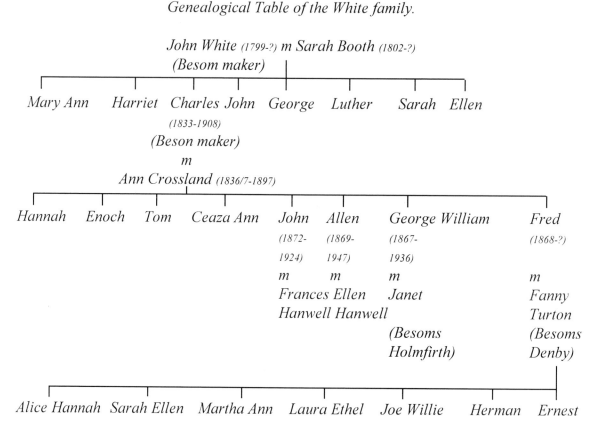

Genealogical Table of the White family.

Tanning and its Offshoots

Tanning was the practice of turning animal hides into leather. The skins were soaked in 'tannin' which was derived from tree bark or vegetable extracts, later mineral salts were used. Once soaked the skins were hung in sheds to dry before being passed to the 'currier' who dressed or treated the leather before being sold. The Post Office directory of 1857 notes that the village tanner was Benjamin Boothroyd, who was part of a large family of tailors.

Cordwainers, Shoemakers and Cobblers

The origin of cordwaining comes from the goat skin leather (cordovan) manufactured in Spain. The cordwainer originally made shoes without heels, and later high boots. This archaic term was the forerunner to shoemaking which incorporated many types of the leather available. The sole leather was hammered to make it hardwaring and the boot or shoe was constructed with the aid of a lasst and a half moon knife. Originally a cottage industry, mechanisation saw its gradual demise in the late 19th century.

Cobblers repaired shoes using materials from many diverse sources, though today the terms 'shoemaker' and 'cobbler' are highly interchangeable. The Hanwell family, aside from running the New Inn. were the village shoemakers for many years (amongst others), the following table will illustrate some of them:

Genealogical Table of Denby Hanwells.

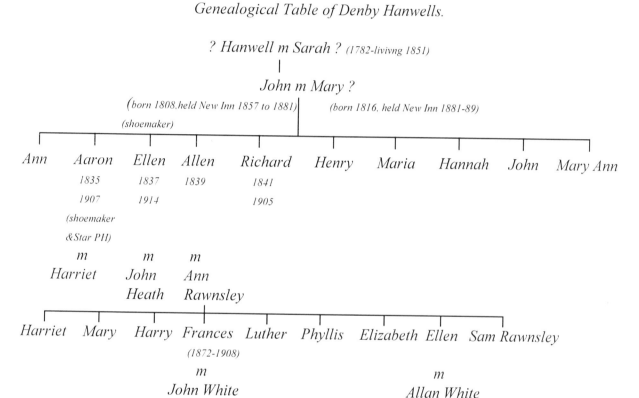

Other families involved with shoemaking were Tyas and Turton.

The saddler was another important offshoot of tanning. The leather was impregnated with grease whilst still wet after tanning in order to make harnesses, saddles and suchlike. The Laundon family, formerly of Syke House were for many years Denby's saddlers.

Surgeons

Two members of the Turton family qualified in this field in the 19th century. Thomas Turton was practising his skills from at least 1838 but between 1866 and 1881 he was succeeded by his son John, who had started out as a chemist.

Surgeons were only as skilled as their instruments and the technology available to them. Sanitation and hygiene were major problems of their time and killer diseases such as measles, cholera and the common cold were difficult to combat resulting in a high mortality rate. The tools of their trade would now look very much at home in a chamber of horrors rather than on an operating bench.

Clay Pits

The clay quarrying activities in Denby took place on the land that is now the Southcroft housing estate. There were originally two pits, the earlier one being across from the former Wesleyan Chapel, the later one being accessed across from Low Fold Farm. Wooden scaffold was constructed to take trucks full of clay along rails, once above the waiting lorry's their contents were tipped into them and transported away. Southcroft was built in the late 1960's, though the clay pits had been disused since the 1940's. Villagers had long been using them as rubbish tips by the time the scaffold was dismantled and the remaining pits filled in. The owner of the pits was Alin Ward, who collapsed and died on Northgate after visiting a privy.

Tailors

The Boothroyd family seem to have been Denby's village tailors for many years. Their job was to cut and create men's clothing, a process possibly brought into the family due to its links with Manor Farm. The family were living here during the textile revolution, and as many farms set up machines for weaving in outbuildings it was only a short step to begin manufacturing clothing from the resulting cloth. Though the Boothroyd's had acquired this skill long before their residence at the farm began.

Genealogical Table of Boothroyd family

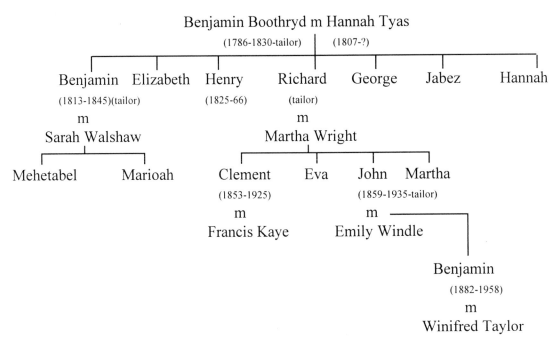

Clement aged 13 and John aged 7 went to live with their Uncle Benjamin at Manor farm in 1866 after their fathers death, their mother having died earlier. John became a tailor following in his families wake. His son, Benjamin broke away from the family trade by becoming a highly skilled stone, marble and wood carver. His work still survives to this day, and can also be seen on some of the tombstones in the churchyard.

The premises for their work included a cottage on Bank Lane which is still owned by a member of the family, Betty Springer.

It was mainly in the top floor of the house that the clothes were made, the Boothroyd's and their employees, who included Lister Peace, working long hours in a profession now almost totally automated.

Right: John Boothroyd and his wife Emily circa 1930.

Benny Boothroyd circa 1910.

Above: A group of workmen, possibly from the clay pits, circa 1925. Standing, left to right; Unknown, Johnny Kilner, unknown, unknown, unknown, Alin Ward, John Gaunt. Front, left to right: unknown, unknown, Clance Morris, unknown.

Below: Annie Heath - who became Sub-Postmistress in Denby after her mothers death in 1947. Photographed here circa 1915.

Miscellaneous

Two ex-slaughter houses exist in Denby today. One is in the grounds of Poplar Villa, the first house on the right heading down Gunthwaite Lane. The other stands detached on the right of Denby Lane just after Upper House. Of course there were others locally, the Barraclough family were involved in this occupation, Isaac working at Exley Gate in 1857. Though the names of Rusby, Morley and Robinson can be added to the list. Norman Naylor ran the detached abattoir on Denby Lane in the mid 20th century.

Charles Bedford & Son ran a rope and twine manufacturers in Lower Denby, during the latter part of the nineteenth century.

The family names of Moore and Ellis were well associated with masonry during the 19th and early 20th centuries, though by the 1940's Jack Hanwell was the monumental mason.

Finally there were numerous coal and quarrying operations in and about the village, John Hargreave & Co. were coal owners in 1866. James Armitage was a farmer and coal owner and George Norton was a quarry owner in 1857 and as we have seen John Micklethwaite was, not only a sub postmaster but also a quarry owner, and farmer!

LEISURE & CELEBRATION

Our forbears lives were very crowded, occupations or trades kept the men busy, working from the early hours until after dark. Women spent much of their time giving birth to and bringing up large family's. Watches, indeed time in general was irrelevant to most, when it was light people got up, when it was dark, they went to bed. They did not live their lives to the clock as we do today.

These people did of course get their free time in these days before wireless and television, village wakes or feasts were very welcome occurrences though employers were seldom pleased at the outcome of such celebrations, for they were known to last many days, resulting in employees not turning up or being unfit for work!

Circus's or fares were also very popular and traditional excuses for having a good time. Entertainment's were varied but one could usually expect to see ballad singers, gingerbread sellers, jugglers, tumblers, freaks, touring menageries, melodramas, travelling showmen of the gypsy variety and even theatre companies. Popular Bank holidays, ie: Whitsuntide, May Day, and Easter would be usual occasions for the appearance of some of the above.

Older forms of village entertainment would certainly have included cock fighting and cock squalling (a rather barbaric game whereby the cockerel was tied to a stake and punters could pay for the privilege of throwing rocks at it. The person that knocked its head off was the winner). Bull baiting and bull running were also popular. In 'running' a local farmer would provide a bull which would then be let loose through the streets, people then chased it and tried to climb on. Finally it would be subdued when it was led onto a bridge, hoisted over, killed and eaten. 'Baiting' involved tying a bull to a stake and letting dogs attack it. If the bull was weak and allowed the dogs to hurt it, it was considered a poor specimen and left to its fate. If the bull fought back, tossing the dogs into the air then it would be deemed a great beast and set free. Dog fighting was also popular, occasionally men would fight with them and then with each other, all for the sake of their own prowess and the gambling public.

Spa Sunday

In the valley of Gunthwaite, below the Hall there is a mineral spring which is supposed to have come from an old silver mine at Ronscliff in Cawthorne, the spring is said to have curative properties. Since the middle ages the spring has been revered, and a blessing of the well ceremony in these early times has led to today's 'Spa Sunday', which takes place on the first Sunday in May.

A procession led by a man with a banner displaying a silver cross, chalice and host would have been watched by such dignitaries as the Bosville's, Burdet's and Micklethwaites, with the lower classes gaining vantage wherever they could.

The man wore a black tunic with a bugle over his shoulder and a chain around his neck, which held a silver plate bearing the insignia of the Abbot of Pontefract. Two Benedictine monks followed in black gowns and hoods. The Abbot himself followed on a pony, attended by the Vicar of Silkstone, Church officials and more monks. With solemnity the Abbot would reach the spring, dismount and bless the water before a muted congregation.

The tradition continued, in the 19th century big gatherings were served by refreshment stalls, the occasion was like a fair, and as many as seven bands have been known there at once. In about 1870, due to rowdiness and trespassing the gatherings were officially stopped, though they did continue into the 20th century, I have been told of activities such as cock fighting taking place here in the 1920's and 30's on this special Sunday.

Today the occasion is still observed, provided the weather is good, an ice cream van is all that remains of the refreshment stalls, but if you are lucky you can still catch one of the local brass bands playing in front of the mill damn.

Coronations and Jubilees

These occasions have always been a popular time for the villagers to party. For instance, after the death of Queen Victoria (1901) it was decided to hold celebrations for the Coronation of Edward VII. Due to his illness in June 1902 the celebrations were abandoned, except for teas given to the old folk and widows at the school and the distribution of mugs and chocolates.

Denby held celebrations to mark the Silver Jubilee of George V in 1935. The day began with the Holy Communion service and continued as listed in the programme on the right.

One event, which began at 11.45 am was the 'Hare and Hounds' Men's running race which started at the New Inn, the runners in the field were as follows:

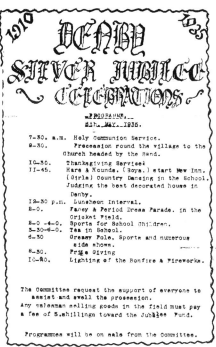

RUNNERS	TRAINERS	COLOURS
Sam Racket	Rawnsley	Mucky Blue
H N Taylor	B Charlesworth	Blood Red
Eli Turton	Fred White	Tangerine
J Rigget	R Armitage	Black & White
Jimmy Pump	G O Tibbits	Marina Green
Teddy Woodhead	J W Heath	White Label
Walt Bobbiner	H Broadhead	Late Buff
Cam Busking	Bob Waldie	Green Un
G Shaw	Jimmy Moore	Daffy Yellow
M Webster	Johnny Moore.	Snow White
Luther Hanwell	Tommy Kilner	Con-Blue
Joe Mosley	Arthur Hudson	Black Hoops
Hugh Beever	A Lockwood	Stone Grey

The Clerk of the course was Bill Dronfield, weigher in T Senior (Butcher).

Unfortunately I do not know who won, yet a read through the names suggests that it must have been an interesting race, without any hint of cheating or gamesmanship! I don't think!

Prizes were also given for the best decorated houses in the village, as can be seen from the photographs overleaf.

Sports events included, country running, skipping, flat races, obstacle race, slow bicycle race, egg & spoon, tennis, and even an 'old man's race'. Prizes for which varied from cricket tackle, clocks, sweaters, and watches for the men to compacts, bread knives and handbags for the women. For the girls skipping, first prize was a scent set, second prize was 'William the Gangster', perhaps a prize for anyone who knows exactly what this was?. The organisers did seem to run out of ideas for the old mans race where both first and second prizes were ash trays!

On 12th May 1937 the village celebrated the Coronation of George VI with an almost identical programme of events, though this time they managed to get a printed programme to sell instead of a type written sheet!

1935 Silver Jubilee, Best Decorated House Competion entrants. Top left; Smithy Hill. Top right; Chapel House - 2nd in competion. Bottom left; The winner showing Ratten Row in the distance to the left.

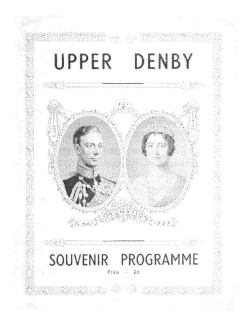

Above right and below; 1935 Upper Denby Coronation Programme.

UPPER DENBY

SOUVENIR PROGRAMME

Price · 2d.

CORONATION CELEBRATIONS.

7·0 a.m.   Holy Eucharist.

9·30 a.m.   Procession to Church.

10·0 a.m.   Church Service.

11·15 a.m.   Jumping Competition in Playing Field

2·0 p.m.   Procession—All in Fancy Dress must Parade.

3·0 p.m.   Judging of Fancy Dress.

3·30 p.m.   Tea, (Children).

4·0—5·30 p.m.   Tea, (Adults).

5·0—8·30 p.m.   Sports in Playing Field.

8·30 p.m.   Prizes presented by Mr. Jonas Kenyon.

10·0 p.m.   Lighting of Bonfire by Miss Hinchliffe.

10·15 p.m.   Fireworks.

FANCY DRESS.

Prizes are offered for the following Classes :

Comic, General, Decorated Bicycles and Perambulators.

DECORATED HOUSES.

Prizes are offered for Best Decorated House,

and also Row of Houses.

Judging of decorations before noon.

SPORTS

To be held in Denby Playing Field

Prizes are given for all Events.

FLAT RACES.

Boys under 8 years.	Girls under 8 years.
,, ,, 12 ,,	,, ,, 12 ,,
,, ,, 16 ,,	,, ,, 16 ,,

JUMPING.

Boys under 10 years.	Girls under 10 years.
,, ,, 16 ,,	,, ,, 16 ,,
,, over 16 ,,	,, over 16 ,,

MEN.

Flat Race, over 50 years.   Obstacle Race.

WOMEN.

Egg and Spoon Three-legged Race.   Obstacle Race.

OPEN.

Sack Race.   Greasy Pole.   Pillow Fight,

Slow Cycle Race.   Tug of War.

Have you received your Surprise Coupon ?

GOD SAVE THE KING.

Denby Feast

The feast would appear in Denby in July and set up in one of two fields. The oldest site was at the end of Milnes Row, in the corner of the field as can be seen from the photograph below. The later site was on land which now plays host to the old folks bungalows and the council estate. The name 'Fairfields' was supplied by Dot Barber, landlady of the George who was asked by Councillor Netherwood for any ideas as to the name of the new site. She suggested that it should reflect the feast or fair which used to be held there, and the rest as they say is history. The Parr family of Penistone brought the bulk of the amusements and the Porter's of Denby added their swing boats, which were kept in the village throughout the winter, until they began touring again the following year. The Porter's lived in the row of houses incorporating what was the Star public house.

Jabus Battye used to bring his roundabout, which was steam powered. This ride could be the one remembered by Jim Barber, which had motorbikes to sit on whilst travelling round on rails, giving the impression to the young that they were driving a motorbike.

The feast appeared on a Friday night and ran through Saturday, closed on Sunday and continued on Monday before packing up and leaving. It was only a small affair, but the villagers became very involved with it, particularly the children. Eventually interest died off and the feast was discontinued due to lack of custom before the second world war.

Denby Feast. Looking down the lane towards The George on the far left, circa 1910.

Jubilee Parade led by Denby Band heading towards Ingbirchworth down Falledge Lane. 1935

Denby Band Hut in the background, possibly the starting point of the May Day festivities, circa 1935.

Denby Band

The band originally used to practice in one of the outbuildings which formed a part of Robinson Lathe. The Pickford family were very involved not only on the playing side but also in the administrative aspects. It was Albert Pickford, who applied to Godfrey Bosville MacDonald for permission to build a wooden band hut, a little way down Gunthwaite Lane on land belonging to the Gunthwaite Estate. MacDonald assented though he did insist that this was all that was built and nothing else. Albert Pickford had lived at Gunthwaite Gate farm since 1912, therefore the band hut was constructed after this.

The band won numerous prizes and were frequently called upon to play at village functions, such as the Gunthwaite and Ingbirchworth Silver Jubilee celebrations in 1935 and it is almost certain that they played in Gunthwaite on Spa Sunday a time or two.

Rivalry existed, of a friendly nature, of course, between local villages, entering competitions and desperately trying to win and retain village pride. The following song gives a good example:

DENBY BRASS

(Composed by Walter Smith)

1 Denby is a pleasant land,
   And they own a little Band.
   But they can't beat Denby Dale,
   Tho' they very seldom fail.

2 When they heard about the Contest,
   Each man said he'd do his best,
   So that they could win a Cup,
   And their faces did light up.

3 Johnny Garratt then comes in,
   Wiping sweat from off his chin,
   And he said to every man,
   "Will you do the best you can?"

4 When the Contest day drew nigh,
   All the lads began to sigh,
   Saying one unto another,
   "Oh! this is a lot of bother",

5 Young Jack Dronfield being small,
   Tried to make himself look tall,
   So he stood upon a buffet,
   And he looked just like Miss Muffet.

6 When the Contest day was done,
   And the prizes were all won,
   Denby Band set out for home,
   Leaving Denby Dale to roam.

7 Poor Johnny Garratt never slept,
   But stayed awake all night and wept,
   Saying to himself in sorrow,
   "I will dress them down to-morrow".

8 Denby Dale with all its fame,
   Put the Denbyites to shame,
   And they all shed many tears,
   Both in madness and with fears.

9 "Never mind" said Johnny Haigh,
   "They are nothing but a plague,
   Wait 'till we have learned to play,
   We will beat them any day".

10 If they would just talk to Cook,
   He would teach them from his book,
   Then like Denby Dale you know,
   To big Contests they could go.

11 Let us hope the next time then,
   That they will play just like men,
   And ins ead of looking sad,
   They will go about quite glad.

12 If I tell you the whole story,
   You will all be in your glory,
   So I think I'll finish here,
   And give them just a word of cheer.

Denby United Silver Prize Band, circa 1930.

The band hut was demolished sometime during the early 1960's and the band was no more, the instruments were reported to be kept at the top of Denby common by Clem Pickford. Although the interest in brass bands has abated somewhat, particularly amongst the young it would still have been a pleasure to listen to them play, perhaps in the George at Christmas time, tunes such as Swain Hark or Pratty Flowers emanating from their instruments.

Denby Club

Denby club was situated on what is now the village green. Newer residents in the village would find it hard to believe that this small triangle of land once played host to not only the club, but two houses and some pig sty's. The club wasn't licensed but did house a billiard table for its patrons, it was more a place to gossip and relax than anything else. Of course being sited next to the house belonging to Jimmy Pump there was always the possibility of unforeseen entertainment, for instance:

Regulars photographed outside the club circa 1925. left to right standing; Kenny Windle Ben Holmes, Arthur Gaunt, Herman White, Bob Beever. Seated; Johnny Haigh, Wilson Moorhouse Ned Beever, Sonny Moorhouse, Visitor.

Some people moved into the house above his and complained to him about the state of his abode. Jimmy then had to spend time clearing away all his rubbish, including his straw filled mattress much to his uncomprehending disgust.

It is possible that after the club closed, the billiard table made its way up to the band hut on Gunthwaite Lane. The band hut did possess a table during the 1950's, though what happened to it when the band hut closed is unknown.

The photograph below shows the site of the club on the far left, along with the residence of Jimmy (Pump) Gaunt, in the centre of the triangle. His home looks like it should be the clubhouse, but I am reliably informed that this was certainly not so in the early 20th century. Before this? who knows?

The photo also shows the Heath grocers and post office and the new house sited on what was the old blacksmiths shop and is dated around 1920.

Football and Cricket

The earliest photograph of a Denby Soccer Team I have been able to discover was taken by James Henry Gaunt, a photographer to whom I am in debt for some of the best photographs in this book. The photograph appeared in the 'Memories of Yesteryear' section of the 'District Chronicle' dated 1966. It depicts Denby Park Avenue (their name at the time) who were winners of the 'Millhouse & District Medal Competition' 1909/10. The team have played in various leagues, including Penistone. The photo was taken outside the George, as with the one printed earlier in this book in the pub's section.

The football team eventually disbanded and wasn't re-started until 1955 when Joe Price, Terry Laundon, Frank Richardson and Arthur Crossland (whose family owned the land which

Those were the days!

PICTORIAL MEMORIES of the happy days of YESTERYEAR, kindly loaned by readers.

Denby A.F.C. — 1909

THE sender of this old photograph does not say whether it was taken on the occasion of the Denby team winning a competition or a championship but the picture was in all probability taken in the ordinary run of all teams who formerly had their photographs taken every season. One or two of the faces (although older) of course are familiar even to us and no doubt residents of Denby will be able to place the players.

Photograph kindly loaned by Mrs. J. T. Gaunt, 4, Richmond Terrace, Denby.

With acknowledgments to the photographer. Mr. James Henry Gaunt, Denby.

110

Upper Denby C.C. 1927. Left to Right, Standing: James Henry Gaunt, Walt Turton, Jack Waldie, John J. (Jack) Pickering, Jimmy Jackson, Fred Roebuck, Bob Waldie, Norman Charlesworth. Left to Right, Seated: Kenny Windle, Joe Turton, Charlie Turton, Ray Charlesworth, Herman White.

was to become the playing field) re-started it, playing in the Penistone league.

The age old game involving willow and leather known as cricket has long been an activity for small villages and Denby was no different. The pitch was originally on Falledge Lane but has since moved to the back of the Church, the photograph above depicts the 1927 team. Village pride in winning was as strong then as it is today.

There were many ways of spending leisure time in Denby, tennis courts used to be at the back of the Church for those so inclined , home pursuits including crafts of all types have always been popular. Village get-togethers were also welcomed. Denby Ladies coffee mornings and fund raising events such as jumble sales will remain with the village into the 21st century and these activities are as popular today as they were in 1916 :

Those were the days !

PICTORIAL MEMORIES of the happy days of YESTERYEAR, kindly loaned by readers.

PICNIC AT UPPER DENBY – 1916 ?

NOW-A-DAYS people go a lot further afield than the next village for outings, but this old photograph, taken about 80 years ago is of a picnic party of members of the Wesleyan Reform Chapel (presumably Denby Dale) taken outside the home of a Mrs. A. Crossland at Upper Denby. A high proportion of the people shown are now dead but they will be remembered by readers in Denby and Denby Dale.

IN DOORWAY: Miss N. Travis, Mrs. J. N. Peace, Willie Hirst, J. A. Riggott.
BACK ROW: R. A. Morris, J. W. Heath, G. Boothroyd, H. Morris.
CENTRE ROW: Mrs. S. Woodhead, Mrs. F. Broadhead, Mrs. H. Heath, Mrs. A. Crossland, Mrs. S. A. Green, Mrs. W. Haigh.
FRONT ROW: Mrs. Gibson, Mrs. B. Senior, Mrs. A. Bedford, Mrs. J. Hirst, Mrs. J. E. Hirst
Photograph kindly loaned by Mrs. L. Nicholson, 3 Miller Row, Denby.

Bonfire night has always been and will always be popular with people, Denby seems to have been celebrating the occasion for many years, in what are now the playing fields, across from the council estate. Organisation under various guises has seen to it that most years food has been available and that a large bonfire has burnt to celebrate the occasion. Provided that mischief night activists haven't already set fire to it!

Boxing Day Hunt

The Rockwood Harriers have for many years been meeting in the car park of the George public house. Throughout the twentieth century, horses, dogs and people have turned up to witness a tradition not always appreciated by today's politically conscious human rights activists, particularly considering the fact that once the horses leave, heading up to Falledge Lane, around dinner time, many are dismounted before actually taking part in a hunt.

Boxing Day Hunt in Denby, circa 1966

Denby Church Youth Club

Church Youth Club, circa 1951.

The youth club began around 1950, instigated by Denby children in association with the Vicar, Norman Moore. The Church had shown a couple of films for the benefit of the villages youth and it had been decided that a youth club should be formed with a view to buying a projector to continue this. Members were drawn only from the Church going fraternity, a fact which annoyed some members of the community and were obliged to pay 1s to attend every Friday night in the school. The members of the club engaged in competitions against neighbouring clubs (not all Church oriented), such as, Kirkburton and Wooldale. The competitions included sports, such as athletics and table tennis and also handicrafts such as woodwork or model making for the boys or needle craft and knitting for the girls. The group were very successful in competition and won many cups. Dances were also held in Denby school. An offshoot of the club was the friendship created between the members, of which one group decided to build some tennis courts at a family home on Denby common. The Church held an annual 'Sale of Work' in November and it was usual to find members of the youth club holed up in the Vicarage making items to sell.

The club also performed playlets and concerts in the Church. One of these involved a song from 'Snow White' called the 'Silly Song', but the words were changed slightly by the Vicar's wife to incorporate a village theme, the following is an incomplete example:

> The collection plate was handed round,
> Said Colin (Crossland) this is certain,
> They can keep their miserly threepenny bits,
> What do you say Mr Turton?
>
> We chased a pig on Ratten Row,
> A big fat buxom fellow,
> It came from Manor Farm,
> Cos it kept shouting Stella.
>
> Hi ho, the tune is done,
> The words don't mean a thing,
> Isn't this a silly song for anyone to sing.

The enterprise seems to have been augmented by the enthusiasm of a generation of children who gradually began to leave the club and enter either National Service or work. Its demise around the late 1950's signalled an end to its achievements but its justification is rewarded in the amount of friendships it augmented, some of which still continue today.

Denby Carnival

In 1962 the village held a colourful carnival, perhaps the residents finally missing the long since departed feast. A parade was organised and competitions, which included fancy dress for both adults and children alike. A scene from this occasion can be found below, depecting the revelers on Ratten Row.

A Scene from the Carnival Held at Denby in 1962.

WORLD WAR 1 TO WORLD WAR 2

The First World War (1914-1918)

W.H.Senior noted that the Victoria Memorial Hall in Denby Dale was converted to a makeshift convalescent home for injured soldiers and sailors, housing 40 beds. It was officially opened in 1916 as the 'Denby and Cumberworth, Skelmanthorpe and Clayton West Military Auxiliary Hospital' which it remained until 28th February 1919, having received 924 patients during its life. The death toll for the Denby and Cumberworth District was 45.

Typhoid in Denby Dale

During 1932 a land drain at Square Wood reservoir became contaminated with the disease culminating in the infection of the inhabitants of the village and the death of ten people. The Denby and Cumberworth Urban District Council organised an appeal fund, the subscriptions of which ranged from business's to private individuals. The reservoir still exists but remains only as a monument to those who died from the lethal water it supplied.

Denby's 'Big Snow'

Often, amongst the older residents of the village a reference will be made to the 'big snow' of 24th February 1933. It was at the time the deepest snow recorded for 50 years. Hence the fact that these people will acknowledge what today is regarded as a heavy snow fall with only a mild, 'the's nobbut a coverin'. Another bad year for snow was 1947.

Right & Below: Scenes taken in the Big Snow of 1933

The Second World War (1939-1945)

Denby was lucky to escape damage from bombs dropped by enemy air-raids. ARP Wardens such as W H Senior and Joe Willie Heath had the duties of enforcing blackouts and assisting in maintaining services after raids. On the night of December 12th 1940, 3 bombs fell in the fields around the village, which were quickly dealt with. The planes that carried them flew on to Sheffield and continued their intended wholesale blitz of the country, the flames as the City burned could be clearly seen from Denby.

Pamphlets were issued, for villagers concerning air-raids advising them to look after their respirators, to be prepared and to keep calm. They advised on how to deal with noxious gasses and even on how to deal with an incendiary bomb.

Denby and its near neighbours made strenuous efforts to provide for the war effort. The 1887 Denby Dale Pie Dish was sold on 20th September 1940 for £72 17s to provide scrap metal.

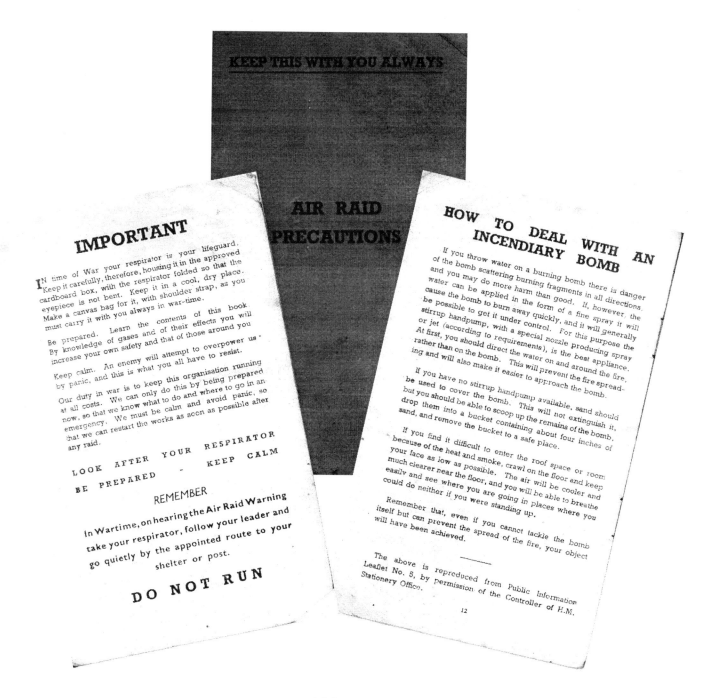

*Above: Cover of the programme produced for
Warship Week 1942.
Right: Wings for Victory Programme cover
1943.*

Denby Dale Urban District held a Warship Week
from 27th February to 7th March 1942, the programme heralded the minimum objective of raising £70,000
for a Motor Torpedo Boat. The actual sum raised was £298,596.

A similar scheme was organised in May, 1943 this one entitled, 'Wings For Victory . The objective
was to provide £80,000 to supply the air force with a plane. The eventual total raised was £182,808.

National Identity cards were issued to the populace as a precautionary measure and food rationing was
introduced in January 1940 for foods which included, butter, bacon and sugar. A points system was
introduced for clothes in June 1942. Although the war ended in 1945, rationing continued, under Attlee's
government until the 1950's, tea was de-rationed in 1952 and sweets in 1953.

Government Evacuation Scheme

As the war with Germany loomed in 1939 a huge operation was mounted to evacuate children from
Britain's cities and towns, moving them to safe areas in the countryside. Each child was labelled and
allowed to take little in the way of personal possessions with them, most had their own gas masks, usually
some spare clothing, toothbrush, comb and a handkerchief along with a bag of food for the day. As
children began to arrive at their temporary homes reports began to come in from country folk, shocked by
the condition of children from city slum areas. Equal shock was expressed by the children at their new
surroundings. For many it was their first sight of cows and other farm animals.

Joe Price was sent from his home in Woolwich in 1941 to a temporary home whilst waiting to be
placed with a new family. His most vivid recollection of this time was the pungent smell of carbolic soap,

used at the home on the kids as soon as they arrived, aged only 3, he little knew that his life was about to change forever.

He arrived by train and was met at the station by a Mrs Norton of Bagden Hall. Mrs Norton was responsible for the 'distribution' of the evacuees and escorted young Joe, by car, to the home of Rob (Robinson) and Amy Graham at Croft Cottages, Lower Denby.

The war dragged on, Joe now being brought up by his surrogate parents, the Graham's alongside their own family. He attended the village school and lived life just as any of the local kids. Letters from his family in Woolwich were regular as his parents tried to keep tabs on their young son.

Joe was 8 or 9 years old (1946/7) when his mother requested that he should go back to Woolwich. The implications for the Graham's were not only apparent but distressing as Joe was by now very much a part of their family and they didn't want to lose him. In the end he did return, for just 9 months. He was very unhappy and indeed became ill, he was taken to see the doctor who decided that he was fretting for Yorkshire and the Graham's. More letters were sent between Woolwich and Denby which eventually concluded with Rob and Amy Graham fetching Joe back to the village.

When he was 18, due to enter the army, and travelling south anyway, Joe became curious to meet his real family and though the visitation occurred he felt no particular emotion towards them, his family now being the Graham's, his home Denby, Yorkshire, in this he would never change. Joe now lives with his wife Monica at the old schoolhouse in Lower Denby, only a few yards from where he was brought up by the Graham's. He is a successful building contractor and is involved in local environmental projects and is as much a part of Denby as the 'George' public house.

Other evacuees to the village of Denby included,
Muriel Towers, who lived with Fred Fawcett and his family,
Lavender Garner, who lived with Vic Gaunt and his family,
Maureen Tickner, who lived with Mrs Town and her family.

The War Memorial

On July 21st, 1923 at 3pm, General Sir Edmund Ironside unveiled the Denby and Cumberworth Urban District Council War Memorial, to commemorate the fallen during the first World War. After the end of the second World War more names were added to it, I shall use the words printed in the pamphlet to finish this chapter:

"They shall not grow old as we who are left grow old;
Age shall not weary them, nor the years dismay:
At the going down of the sun and in the morning;
We will remember them."

A WANDER AROUND MID 20TH CENTURY DENBY

Within the context of this book we have examined as much of the villages history as possible, but, it would be impossible to include all the people and characters so essential to its development and so to finish I will try to include as many as possible by taking a metaphorical walk around Denby in the mid 20th century. I am sure older residents will be familiar with the names and habits that will follow and that they will be ready to correct me should the need arise.

Finally, I must admit to a little poetic licence, but of course, for a set of coincidences such as follows to occur in a couple of hours would be fortuitous in the extreme.

It is a warm and sunny Saturday afternoon, the fields roll around us, undulating squares of varying greens and browns, broken only by the dry stone walls, many of which were built at the time of the enclosure awards in 1802. We are standing at the entrance to Gunthwaite Gate farm, sited on the border between Denby and Gunthwaite, the home of the Pickford family. Dog daisies litter the fields which surround two agricultural traction engines that are pulled slightly off the road. We begin our walk up Gunthwaite Lane, heading away from the farm, passing the seat for weary walkers on our left. Skylarks, hover above, occasionally swooping, then effortlessly climbing back up and floating gracefully in the light breeze. Across to our right are playing fields, a sandpit, seesaw and football goal which entertain the local kids to great extent. Beyond is the tip of the Clay Pit, once owned by Alin Ward now used as a rubbish tip by the villagers. A little further on and the wooden band hut comes into view. A faint but audible brass tune emanates from within, due to the efforts of railway linesman, Jim Harley, conducting the Denby prize band.

Denby Band in front of the Band Hut, circa 1930.

As we continue we find we have to tread very carefully around hot tar as the road is being repaired. Jim Slater with his steam engine and Burdett Haigh with his red, Bedford lorry, loaded with sand and pebbles are sweating profusely in the sun as both lend a hand in using the tar sprayer. A gang of local kids, gradually getting splattered with tar add to the proceedings. The hot tar is sprayed onto the road, completely covering it, pebbles are then thrown on, as evenly as possible with shovels. Jim then starts up the roller, black smoke pluthering from the chimney and moves backwards and forwards over the new area until it is flat and hard. Once completed the team will move forward and repeat the procedure until the job is done.

A few assured strides further and we are at the end of the Lane, where we find a bus turning round, backing into Gunthwaite lane to return back up the village and on into Huddersfield. To our left is the home of Mirfield school teacher, Norman Peace, a historian of some note. The house now known as 'Poplar Villa' was once called 'Spion Cop'. Spion Cop was a peak in South Africa, which was captured by British troops at the orders of General Buller. Once attained the troops were subjected to heavy attack from the 'Boers', the date was 24th January 1900. Many hundreds of soldiers died an both sides which resulted in a temporary armistice, which allowed both armies to collect and bury their dead. The British forces then withdrew. How the house became so named is unknown, though one presumes that a veteran of the battle would be the most likely author.

Across the road we can hear chatter from the patrons of the New Inn as workers quench their thirsts with the golden brew. As we draw nearer we pause to examine the notice board on the wall, detailing the selection of the cricket team for today's match in the Red Triangle League

1. Dennis Pell	2. Carl Taylor	3. David Flack
4. Duncan Ross	5. John Gaunt	6. Frank Burdett
7. Percy Wadsworth	8. Fred Barden	9. Keith Herbert
10. Oliver Marsh	11. Colin Crossland	

It is to be hoped that wicket keeper, Barden, has finished his milk deliveries, which he achieves on a bike with a basket attachment! As we round the back of the pub, on the Ratten Row we see a lorry marked Hammonds Ales delivering its weekly stock, Hammonds having taken over from Seth Seniors Breweries. Percy Cartwright, the landlord is supervising the unloading. The first house after this is occupied by Mrs Smithson, on a whim we call in and buy a quarter of Dolly Mixtures from her kitchen table. Groceries can also be bought further on at the Co. Op, run by Teddy Higson, and also at the other side of the road, at the red brick house owned by Arthur Turton, who sells veg. & salad, although be careful to ask for a 'bob' of lettuce rather than a bobs worth or your arms will be full. Having finished our sweets we call at the entry on our left to see Clance Morris where we buy some more sweets, boiled ones this time and spend a moment or two whilst he reminisces about his mining days, abruptly ended by an accident which broke his back. We leave Clance listening to the wireless and continue past the homes of Horace Knowles, an auctioneer, Edward Hudson, butcher at the Co. Op, Arthur Laundon, Norton's textiles, and Bob Pontefract a baker, with his bread wagon parked outside. At Kilncroft House we turn and wave cheerily to Harry Battye, a part time wireless repair man and look up the lane to Manor farm, where we see Colin Crossland's horse drawn milk float parked in the yard. A couple of Milk churns are still aboard it, though the milk was transferred from these into smaller ones for taking into the houses, where long handled jugs measured out pints or gills at the customers request. By chance the owner of the farm, Math Webster is coming towards us, herding his cows in for milking, back from Long Lane. Distinctive in his smock, he brandishes a walking stick, gently persuading the cows to behave and move in the right direction, he greets us as we pass.

We continue down Long Lane, passing Joe Turton, having a day off from Naylor's clay pit, hard at work, proudly mowing his beautiful lawn at Rock House. Approaching us from Lemon Acre are the Pickford's, with a full cart of freshly cut hay, drawn by their giant cart horse, George. We now turn back on ourselves and cross the style into Tom Seniors field where we are suddenly under attack from a gander and so a short run is necessary to avoid its eager beak, we should have brought the dog with us!

We come out into back lane, opposite the house once owned by Sam (Racket) Rawnsley, a name, apparently, thoroughly deserved! To our left is Coal Pit Lane, now silent and overgrown as the more familiar sound of hob-nail boots tramp its course no more. We continue down to the joiners and undertakers run by Joe Willie Heath. Entering the yard before us is 'Owd Bennet', of 'Fagin' like appearance his scruffy dog yaps cherpily by his side. The shop is a regular meeting place for locals and he regales them with a tune on his tin whistle. Three or four more people can be glimpsed inside 'calin' with each other.

As we reach the end of the lane we turn into Post Office Row where we see two people going about their business. One is Lena Heath, holding a wireless battery on her way to see George Rotherforth to have it re-charged, so there must be something good on the wireless tonight. The battery, known as an accumulator was like a car battery in appearance, made of glass, about 4 inches square and 10 inches tall, filled with acid and distilled water, with red and black terminals on top. The whole fitted into a metal carrier for transportation to someone with a charger and, obviously, electricity. Not many homes had electricity and they were lit by gas or oil lamps.

The other figure is that of Joe Willie White, just leaving his cottage with his trusty rabbitting dog and 12 bore shotgun broken over his shoulder, wearing his familiar loose collar shirt, minus collar with a scarf tied round his neck, cowboy style. He's probably going down Gunthwaite Lane to the railway banking.

A little further on and we see two vans parked outside the post office and grocer's. The first which is just pulling away belongs to the post office, the red Morris Minor driven by Milton Morris has the familiar double back doors with a bar lock on the outside. The second is that of J. Wood Ltd, confectioners, delivering to the shop. We enter the shop to buy some stamps and are greeted by Annie Heath. She stands behind a long counter, perched on it are a set of scales and a small display cabinet. The walls and floors and even shelves suspended from the ceiling are arranged with foodstuffs. A free space on the wall by the door is covered by a poster advertising a:

Whistdrive and dance in Denby school, proceeds to the Church, at 8pm tonight, where the Serenaders band will be playing.

There is also a bill for Penistone pictures, where entry to see Johnny Weismuller in Tarzan costs : 1/3d (7p), 1/6d (7 ½p), and 2/6d (12 ½p) for the balcony. We buy our stamp and bid Annie good-day as she turns to deal with the van driver.

Turning left out of the door we pass what used to be the Star public house, now occupied privately by Mrs Town and on past the George public house where we can see through the windows, Frank Widdowson serving customers from behind the bar. The wooden doors into the barn at the top of the pub yard are open and a large dog lays in wait for over eager patrons. A little further on and we can see one of the former sites of the now abolished Denby feast, to our right, Fred Nicholson, retired farmer, and now caretaker of Denby Band hut, is hard at work in his allotment. He is watching warily at the antics of a group of noisy children playing under the gantry of the clay pit, he shakes his head in resignation at me and smiles his good-day. Beyond this is the ramshackle caravan used as a lodging by 'Owd Bennet', whose real name may have been 'Kettle' housed on land belonging to the Pickford's of Denroyd farm.

Even further down the hill is Pinfold House, built in 1795 on the site where there were actually two pinfold's for rounding up stray cattle, but we turn and travel back up the main road past Milnes Row, noticing Mrs Grange smoking a clay pipe, sitting outside with her daughters, Ginny and Emma.

At the end house, Rafe Barber is tending his poultry. Looking across we can see the club, housing a billiard table for its patrons, walled in with the residence of Jimmy 'Pump' Gaunt, on the triangle of land, opposite the former site of the Barraclough blacksmiths shop, next door to the post office, now demolished to make way for the residence of Ernest and Dorothy Heath. Oh, and a piece of advice, if you meet Jimmy Gaunt, remember not to call him 'Pump'!!

Above the club is the building which was used as a Wesleyan Chapel, now converted into a home by Joe Willie Heath. The gate up to the house is supported by two large stones, reputed to have once been the Denby stocks. On the road in front of them is Henry Broadhead sorting out his newspapers before setting off on his rounds. The local bobby, Mr Glazebrook, comes past us up the lane and turns into his path, ready for his lunch. Also on our right as we continue up Denby Lane is the monumental mason's, and

Mrs. Grange, seated, with her family, Ginny on the left, Emma on the right. Circa 1941.

Jack Hanwell himself is outside putting the finishing touches to a gravestone.

We make our way on past the home of Joe Windle and on to Highfield farm, residence of the Charlesworth's where we decide to take a short cut through the yard to check on the cricket scores. In the field beyond we see the scoreboard on the pavilion reads that Denby are struggling on 77 for 7, no change there! play has in fact stopped as a rather lusty blow has sent the ball into the orchard and half the team are searching for it, still its better than landing it in the graveyard!

We nip out of the cricket field and carry on past the slaughter house and butchers belonging to Norman Naylor. Coming out of the entrance to Tom Priests farm on the left is Tom Moxon. He is driving what appears to be a full load in his cattle wagon, probably on his way to Penistone. Approaching us, coming down the lane is Fred Bower in his wagon, shouting his familiar cry,'lampoil' referring to the large drum of paraffin attached to the back of his vehicle. As we near the Church we see Rev. Moore crossing the road from the vicarage to attend to some matter in the Church, and we hear someone testing the school bell, normally rung by Miss Thompson, the headmistress, or Miss Close to signal the beginning of school for the day when both would be outside to make sure the children were lined up ready to enter the building.

Tom Moxon's advert placed in the 1954 Penistone Almanack.

Denby Schoolchildren outside the long window, before it was extended to playground level, circa 1946.

The bell just outside the front door is attached to a black rope inside the classroom and is rung at the start and end of each day and also at playtime, scholars are usually permitted to ring it by the teachers. Miss Close teaches baby and standard one classes, Miss Thompson standards 2,3 and 4 all in the same room, where students may use ink or pencil to make notes in their jotters.

Just past the school we reach the small reservoir, a little way up the common. Here again we cross the fields, past the farm belonging to Reg Mosley and over towards Mosley Roughs, on to the top of Broom fields. Briefly we take in the stunning rural landscape, looking out over Cumberworth, 40 steps, High Flatts and Denby Dale before heading back into the village through Long Lane wood. Looking left we

Left: Annie Heath and friend fetching water from Haley Well, circa 1935.

Below: Street Urchins with the village Bobby, Smithy Hill circa 1940.

can see Breeches field or close where the kids go sledging in Winter snows and as we walk up the actual lane we notice the hollow known as the 'basin' which was dug out at the time of the building of the railways and used as filler for the viaduct. Quite a way behind this, in the middle of a field is Haley Well, used by the villagers in time of need.

We come back into the village via Bank Lane turning down by the green and past the cottages on Northgate or 'Flying Poker Street' as it was affectionately known! We would

have continued the walk by using the snicket known as 'Shedley' just before reaching the Ratten Row, but unfortunately thirst has overtaken us and so we nip down the snicket between the joiners low shop and the cottage adjoining what was the Star, which brings us out, almost at the entrance to the George, where we finish with a pint of best.

Aerial view of Upper Denby, showing the George Public House in the centre circa 1960.

POSTSCRIPT

Since the war years many of the people and buildings so familiar to the older residents of the village have disappeared. The 'old Denbiers' have dwindled in number, being replaced by newcomers, attracted by the site and situation of the village. Its close proximity to Barnsley, Wakefield and Huddersfield, alongside its easy access to the M1 motorway make it an ideal place to live in this commuter age.

New housing has been built, the council estate, named Fairfields and the Southcroft housing estate alongside many other detached and semi-detached abodes.

Only one shop remains in the village, that of Peter Homes the butcher at the top of Gunthwaite Lane, there is no Post Office or general store nor even a newsagents. Harry Heath, the last in a long line of joiners is now semi-retired and the working farms have grown fewer in number as barns and outbuildings are re-developed into private homes. The village is still alive because of its changes, most of which would confound former occupants from the 19th century and before, yet it is now considered to be one of the most beautiful villages in Britain, an accolade achieved from its high placing in the annual competition to find the same.

Bonfire night is still observed up in the playing fields, the Rockwood Harriers still meet on Boxing Day morning at the George and Denby Ladies hold a jumble sale every May, to help pay for the old folk's annual dinner. The fish and chip shop run by Mr & Mrs Bert Fisher on Denby Lane, across from today's village green was closed in 1939 and the street sellers and gypsies have long since gone, leaving Denby Dale as the nearest centre for local amenities. Though mobile grocers and a library still entertain at least the older folk in the village.

Cricket and Football teams still play at the back of Manor Farm though the tennis courts are gone, but the footpaths and bridle ways, once so central to the travel and communications of the village are still much used by ramblers and dog walkers, though many know the routes the names may be unfamiliar to some ie: Gladehouses, Daffy Wood and Forty Steps.

The relatives of the old Lords of the Manor are still here, though of their powerful neighbours the Bosville's nothing remains, though it would be perhaps interesting to know what Aymer Burdet III, would have thought of the village and its occupants now.

All the people of today's village are in debt to their predecessors considered in these few pages for the shape and station of the village today. Many will be oblivious to its rich and diverse history, though it is a history repeated throughout the country, only the characters are different.

Italian historians coined the term 'microhistory' for the study of Local History, they saw it as 'attempting to see the world in a grain of sand'. Most villages were caught up in national events, the problem is finding evidence of this. For instance, at present I do not know whether the Burdet's played any part in the 'Wars of the Roses', whether the civil strife in the 12th century between Stephen and Matilda had any effect on Denby or indeed many other interesting scenarios.

In most cases the evidence has not survived and the truth will never be known. The statement taken at the trial of Susan Hinchcliffe and Ann Shillitoe in 1674 has disappeared, as has the muster roll for the defence of the country at the time of the Spanish Armada. The details of Bishop Longley's visitation to the church and his well known thought, that it was 'in such a filthy and ruinous state' may well never have been written down, as the Rev. Joseph Hunter was writing about Denby only a few years before rebuilding commenced, the evidence may well have been oral only.

Therefore we are left with written accounts of these developments by historians of the past, their interpretation is in many cases all that remains and it is upon these facts that I have tried to build. With luck, in my own lifetime I may be able to glean a better and more substantial picture of the village, either due to my own efforts or perhaps to the efforts of others who I hope will be encouraged to take up this most absorbing of pursuits by the publication of my results so far.

Appendix 1
Select listing of regular Denby surname meanings

ARMITAGE	derived from hermitage, place in Staffs.
BARRACLOUGH	dell with a grove.
BEAUMONT	lovely hill, of Norman origin.
BEAVER OR BEEVER	beautiful view, compare with town of Beverley.
BLACKBURN	black stream, and a number of places.
BOOTH	hut, shed or shelter.
BOOTHROYD	a clearing with huts or sheds.
CLAYTON	place in the clay, or place with good clay for pottery, or derived from place - Clayton (West).
CHARLESWORTH	2 parts, Charles derived from Germanic Emperor, Charlemagne, Worth is an enclosure, fence or homestead.
CHALLENGOR	plaintiff, challenger, accuser.
COLDWELL	cold spring or stream.
CROWTHER	fiddler, from the Welsh 'crwth'.
DICKINSON	son of Richard, comparative with Dixon.
DYSON	follower of Bacchus, or son of person who's name began with D.
ELLIS	form of Elias, in Welsh, charitable, benevolent.
FIRTH	woodland.
GAUNT	either the Belgian city, or bleak, lean and haggard.
GRAHAM	homestead of Granta, a grinner, snarler or grumbler, also a gravelly home stead.
HAWKESWORTH	2 parts, Hawks, from rapacity, or keeping hawks, or paying them as rent, Worth, enclosure, fence or homestead.
HAIGH	enclosure, paddock, various spellings.
HORN(E)	either horn shaped hill, gable, pinnacle or land in a river bed.
HANWELL	2 parts, Han, possibly derived from person named Johann, Well is well, spring or stream.
HUDSON	the son of a man named Richard(hud).
HEATH	dweller on the heath.
HIRST	copse, hill, wooded hill.
JESSOP	form of Joseph, of Italian Jewish origin ie, Giuseppe.
KILNER	worker at a kilne, lime burner.
LAUNDON	form of lavender, washer woman, launderer.
LOCKWOOD	enclosed wood and a place.
MOORHOUSE	house in a moor, or fen.
MOORE	the moor, from Latin maurus, name of 6th century Saint.
MOSLEY	2 parts, first is marsh or bog, second is wood/clearing.
MARSHALL	horse servant, farmer, groom, horse doctor.
MICKLETHWAITE	big thwaite, a thwaite was a clearing, meadow etc.
MALLINSON	son of Mary, ie-wished for a child, Hebrew origin.
MARSDEN	boundary valley.
MOXON	son of a person named Mog or Mogga.
MILNES	of or at the mill.

POLLARD	possibly crop head, or big(large) head.
PRIEST	relates to the word, presbytr, the Greek word for elder.
PEACE	of Pace, meaning peace or concord.
ROBINSON	son of Robert or Robin.
RUSBY	possibly a bed of rushes.
SHAW	copse, thicket, small wood.
SWIFT	literally swift or quick.
SLATER	a person who covers roofs with slates, or sheep pasture.
SENIOR	either Lord (as in Manor), or senior as opposed to junior or swagger.
TURTON	Thors farm literally from the pagan God of thunder.
TYAS	of German origin.
WOOD	wood, or of the wood etc.

(NB: many surnames were spelt in a variety of ways).

Bibliography

1)	Penistone Almanac 1954		
2)	Penistone Almanac 1984		
3)	A Stroll Round Denbi	A.Kenyon/P.Thorpe	
4)	The History of Kirkburton & Graveship of Holme	Henry Moorhouse	
5)	South Yorkshire Volume 2	Rev. Joseph Hunter	
6)	Historical Notes on Skelmanthorpe & District	Fred Lawton	
7)	The Boer War	Eversley Belfield	Pen & Sword
8)	The Making of Barnsley	Brian Elliot	Wharncliffe
9)	Tales of Witches & Sorcery	Ken Radford	Chancellor Press
10)	Doomsday Book Volume 1 & 2	Gen.Ed. John Morris	Philimore
11)	Yorkshire From AD1000	David Hey	Longman
12)	Aspects of Barnsley	Vera Nicholson	Wharncliffe
13)	A History of Denby Dale Urban District	W H Senior	Denby Dale UDC
14)	Doomsday Book to Magna Carta	A L Poole	Oxford
15)	Celt & Saxon	Peter Beresford Ellis	Constable
16)	Modern British History	Cook & Stevenson	Longman
17)	Success in British History	Peter Lane	John Murray
18)	Oxford Illustrated History of the British Monarchy	Canon & Griffiths	Oxford
19)	The Age of Arthur	John Morris	Weidenfeld&Nicholson.
20)	The Fury of the Northmen	John Marsden	BCA
21)	Oxford Illustrated History of Roman Britain	Peter Salway	Oxford
22)	Plain Country Friends	Bower & Knight	Wooldale Friends
23)	Historical Britain	Eric S Wood	Harvill
24)	History Today Companion to British History	Various authors	Collins & Brown.
25)	Divine Magic	Andre&Lynette Singer	Boxtree
26)	The Kingdom of Northumbria	N J Higham	Alan Sutton
27)	Penguin Dictionary of Surnames	Basil Cottle	Penguin
28)	Ecclesiastical History of of the English People	Bede	Penguin
29)	The Saxon Chronicle	Rev. J Ingram	Studio Editions
30)	In Search of the Dark Ages	Michael Wood	BBC
31)	Prehistoric Settlements	Robert Bewley	Batsford
32)	Iron Age Britain	Barry Cuncliffe	Batsford
33)	Viking Age England	Julian D Richards	Batsford
34)	The John Goodchild Collection - Wakefield		
35)	Huddersfield Local History Library		
36)	Burkes Peerage		
37)	Wakefield County Archives		
38)	West Yorkshire Archaeology Service		
39)	History of Penistone	John Ness Dransfield	
40)	Victoria County History Vols. 1,2,&3		
41)	John Lelands Itinerary	John Chandler	Alan Sutton
42)	The Life of Oliver Heywood	Joseph Hunter	
43)	Comptons Encyclopaedia Vol.3		
44)	A Further History of Penistone	PenistoneWEA History Group.	
45)	Denbigh Castle	CADW Welsh Historic Monuments	

Epitaph

Even such is time, which takes in trust
Our youth our joys, and all we have,
And pays us but with age and dust;
Who in the dark and silent grave,
When we have wandered all our ways,
Shuts up the story of our days:
And from which earth, and grave and dust,
The Lord shall raise me up, I trust.

Walter Raleigh.